1 & 2 *Work on the Ground:* Half-turn on the forehand at the walk.

3 *Correct Halt :* The horse straight and square in *ramener* and on the bit.

The Rising Trot: Note the engagement of the hind leg.

5 *Half-Turn on the Forehand at the Walk :* Responding to right-leg action, the off-hind is crossing the near. The off-fore serves as a pivot and is marking its own beat. The rider is straight.

6 *Half-Turn on the Forehand :* A common fault. The rider looks in the direction of his acting leg, causing his weight to be placed on the right buttock, while the horse's haunches are shifted to the left. The weight should be on the left buttock.

7 *Half-Turn on the Haunches to the Left :* Horse straight; good crossing of the forelegs; the near hind, which is the pivot here, clearly maintains the cadence of the walk.

8 *Half-Turn on the Haunches to the Left :* The horse engaged in the phase immediately following the one shown in the preceding photograph, the near-hind having advanced further beneath the body and the near-fore leaving the ground in order to move left. The neck is straight. The rider uses barely taut reins to drive the horse to the left by a counter-rein effect, while his right leg checks the haunches; no need for urging or restraint since the horse is in the proper balance.

9 *Circle on the Left Rein:* The right shoulder pushed slightly forward keeps the rider facing the direction of movement.

10 *Circle on the Left Rein:* This photo was taken at the same place on the circle as the other and from the same angle. The right shoulder is not pushed forward and the rider is behind the movement.

11 *Circle on the Left Rein:* The same circle, taken from a different angle. Not only the right shoulder but the rider's entire body is now shown to be behind the movement.

12 *True Canter on the Near Lead:* Though the rider's legs and hands are passive the normal action of the gait drives the horse's haunches to the left. Note the position of the haunches in relation to the rider's left and right leg, neither of which has moved.

13 *True Canter on the Off Lead:* Haunches now driven naturally to the right. Note that this and the preceding photo have been taken at precisely the same time and instant of the canter.

14 *Counter Canter:* Serpentine. The horse is cantering on the near lead, photographed where the counter-canter loop is at its sharpest. Head and neck are perfectly straight, horse and rider totally at ease.

15 *Counter Canter:* Trying to force the horse. Taken at exactly the same place as before with the horse in both pictures at the third time of the canter.

16 *Rein Back:* The horse raises his head, thereby making a hollow back. This is aggravated by the rider who is crushing the small of his back down into the saddle. Inevitably, though the rein back is a diagonal gait of two time, the near-hind has reached the ground, while the off-fore is still in the air.

17 *Rein Back:* Most of the rider's weight rests on the stirrups, leaving the seat free to accompany the movement. The horse's head is lower than in the previous photograph. Although the backward step is a little shorter the two limbs of the (near) diagonal retreat evenly.

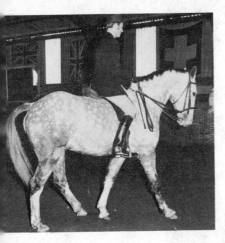

18 *Rein Back:* Here the rider relieves the horse's back even more and the head has been brought down. As a result the horse reins back with greater ease. The step just executed by the near diagonal is longer than before but the retreat of its two limbs remains even. While teaching the rein back, the rider should act as shown in 17 and 18. Only after the movement itself has considerably improved can both horse and rider afford an entirely classical position.

19 *Left Shoulder-In:* The horse is only slightly bent, corresponding to the large circle on which he had been travelling prior to this movement. Note the uniform bend from poll to dock. Photographed at the precise moment of leaving the circle in order to move to the right.

20 *Left Shoulder-In:* This photograph taken of the same movement a moment later shows even more clearly the evenness of the bend. Note the engagement and crossing of the near hind.

Left Shoulder-In : The most common fault is for the bend of the neck
t to correspond to that of the body.

22 *Left Shoulder-In:* Here, as before, the bend of the neck is excessive, but now also the poll is twisted, which is shown by one ear being higher than the other.

An Expert's Guide to
BASIC DRESSAGE

Jean Froissard

Translated by Lily Powell-Froissard

Melvin Powers
Wilshire Book Company

12015 Sherman Road, No. Hollywood, CA 91605

THOMAS NELSON AND SONS LTD
36 Park Street London W1Y 4DE
PO Box 18123 Nairobi Kenya

THOMAS NELSON (AUSTRALIA) LTD
597 Little Collins Street Melbourne 3000

THOMAS NELSON AND SONS (CANADA) LTD
81 Curlew Drive Don Mills Ontario

THOMAS NELSON (NIGERIA) LTD
PO Box 336 Apapa Lagos

THOMAS NELSON AND SONS (SOUTH AFRICA)
(PROPRIETARY) LTD
51 Commissioner Street Johannesburg

This book first published 1971
© Jean Froissard 1971
ISBN 0-87980-219-7

CONTENTS

ACKNOWLEDGEMENTS

The Plates are by courtesy of Capt. C. Kendall of the Benenden Riding Establishment who enabled the author to be shown in these photographs mounted on 'Dromoland Castle'.

ILLUSTRATIONS

Photographs taken by Leslie Lane at Captain C. E. Kendall's Benenden Riding Establishment.

Chapter 1

'TO DRESS A HORSE'

'*A New Method and Extraordinary Invention to Dress Horses and Work them According to Nature by the Subtlety of Art*', by William Cavendish, Duke of Newcastle, London, 1667.

The Duke was not an early wag, preocccupied with 'decency for animals', he simply used the equestrian term, 'to dress', for the word, training, as did everyone else in his time. The verb has vanished from the English language but the noun, 'dressage', has received a frightful buffeting. Dressage to the average modern rider is a competitive event. Yet dressage means nothing except training, the training of the horse, not the rider, who is supposed to know what he is doing before he ventures to teach his horse. The French word for breaking in is *débourrage* (characteristically originating in the ordinary, everyday sense of cleaning, scraping, smartening up). The French for training is *dressage*, describing not only the period following the breaking in, but also, as does training, the entire education.

The title of the Newcastle book is, in itself, a capsule lesson in the meaning of dressage, as it adds, 'and work them according to nature by the subtlety of art'. It could not be better expressed, defining the very essence of the craft of dressage and, ultimately, the art of *haute-école*, as distinguished from

1

circus riding. Both exclude all but natural movements, performed by the horse spontaneously at liberty. Dressage proposes to stylize them and *haute-école* carries them to perfection.

Haute-école, then, is the 'higher education' of a horse, provided by 'teachers of high academic standing'. It should not be confused, as it too often is, with what we call dressage, and the French call, *basse-école* (low, as opposed to high, school), the horse's 'secondary education'. It is with this secondary level that this book is concerned.

We will begin at the beginning, acquire the proper horse, then learn to train him, step by step. The 'dressage test' is just exactly what it declares itself to be: a test of training. So let us think of training only, until we have done the work up to the point where we may submit it for the consideration of a judge. Then we will begin to think of what to do and not to do in the arena. Go along with me without skipping and I do not think you will regret it; for there is no such recipe for instant dressage as 'take a few pupils, add an equal amount of horses, place all of it into a school, pour over it the counsel of a teacher and let steep for three or four days'. On the other hand, dressage is, as I said, a craft and thus it can be taught and learned in simple terms by relatively simple means, provided the student has already a good seat, steadiness, independence of aids and a certain feeling, called equestrian tact. Besides this he must be willing to work. If it is true that one can lead a horse to water but cannot make him drink, it is true that one can teach a rider but cannot make him learn. Personal work is all the more essential in horsemanship, on any level, because riding is not a purely mental skill. It cannot be absorbed entirely just by reading, listening, or even watching.

I am myself an avid reader and writer of equestrian books

and articles and so I have no axe to grind when I warn you off excessive armchair equitation. My point is that if you cannot feel what you do not understand, you cannot understand what you do not feel. Both capacities develop together. I shall try, from chapter to chapter, to make you understand what you begin to feel, if you will try to feel what I give you to understand.

Shopping for a Horse With a good seat, steadiness, independence of aids and a measure of equestrian tact you can enter into dressage, aiming to ride a horse competently in the elementary tests. But for this purpose you do not want an entirely green horse, which would require the employment of an experienced trainer if he was not to be spoilt. On the other hand, you do not wish to perform, like a couple of wind-up toys, with a mount trained from A to Z by someone more knowledgeable than you; anyhow, it cannot really be done. Neither do you want a too highly trained horse; you would not speak or understand each other's language and the end would be the ruin of both of you. What you do want is a six- to seven-year-old having had as good and rational a basic training as you should have received.

This kind of training is easily recognizable when you try the horse under saddle. He should be quiet, not sluggish, go forward freely without need of whip or spur, turn as easily to the left as to the right, and at all three gaits accept the contact with the bit on normal rein tension. He must look where he is going, not coiling his neck as though searching for a four-leaved clover, nor raising it to study cloud formations. Whilst keeping definite contact with the hand, he should not pull at it or expect it to carry his head for him, nor must he move his head about at halt or in action. A jaw opening and closing constantly, or a lolling tongue, eliminates him from the picture, because these difficulties are almost impossible to overcome.

So he is well-behaved and apparently well-intentioned; but will his spirit and conformation let him progress along the path you have chosen? If he is to become a dressage horse he must be reasonably calm. It is possible for a very skilful trainer to get some use out of a high-strung, skittish, timid sort of horse in time, but even he will never be safe from unpleasant surprises in the arena.

Though there are fine and even outstanding mares on the dressage scene in general it is well to remember that geldings tend to be more even-tempered. This much for character.

Physically, he should, as any riding horse, have good natural balance. For *manège* work we want to see the top of the croup slightly lower than the top of the withers. This is the ideal, although we may accept withers and croup of equal height if all else is equal. Never, however, buy a potential dressage horse who stands higher behind than in front.

An easy, quick way of judging conformation is to check that the distance between the back of the withers and the front of the croup is reasonably short and that the distance between the point of the shoulder and the last false rib is fairly long. Most important, however, is the difference between these two distances: the greater the difference, the better the horse.

This standard of proportions almost guarantees several qualities which, when examined separately, require more judging experience than most of you will have at this stage. If the distances in themselves and their relationship to each other are good, we usually find a good withers, not only high but (this is essential) stretching well back; not too much length in back and loins; a long, sloping shoulder, endowing the horse with good balance, and a deep chest.

Having examined those two distances and their relationship, we can look at the neck, which should be rather long, well muscled, but not thick, and carry a head of proportionate size. Too heavy a head makes the horse weigh on the hand and robs him of elegance whilst thick jowls prevent proper head carriage. Excellent points, however, are a neck well hung on (in other words, well oriented in emerging from the body) and a head well set onto this neck. A ewe-neck disqualifies outright, no amount of work will set it right. If you are curious to know in what position the fully trained horse under the saddle will eventually carry his neck at walk, trot and canter, you only need to note where he carries it naturally when trotting at liberty.

While you have him at the trot, look at his tail. Normal carriage indicates energy and good muscle tone at the top line. If it is too high there is stiffness on the top line and possibly some incorrect muscular development. If he clamps his tail between his buttocks it is a certain indication of stiffness somewhere and obviously it will affect his action.

Look at his way of going at the trot; profile, front and rear. If he crosses his legs, do not take him. If he dishes you will have trouble and he will never reach extended gaits. Ideally, his way of going should be true, but a little turning in of the toes may be overlooked.

Concerning the formation of the legs at the halt, it is important that the horse should stand square on all four feet. Avoid sickle hocks, or a horse whose forelegs slant to the rear at halt and come almost beneath the centre. Finally take a good look at his feet – 'no foot, no 'oss.'

Then pay some general attention to elegance and size. In dressage tests, elementary or advanced, elegance is a factor and judges tend to be impressed by it. Size does not necessarily make for elegance but it enhances whatever there is of it. The gaits of a very small horse tend to convey a more cramped appearance, especially when following a taller entry whose speed-ups and slow-downs, though not actually better, will look more generous. Seek as much elegance, then, as you can afford, without sacrificing the more basic qualities.

Now have him vetted; the expense may save you far more costly surprises. Only the veterinary surgeon can assure you that your prospective purchase, who travels as much on his heart and lungs as on his legs, is organically sound. And only he can confirm that he has good eyesight. This is an important point, for often the horse scared of a tree is the one who does not recognize it for what it is.

To sum up, we want a horse sound in mind and body, of harmonious proportions, somewhat elegant bearing and with considerable mettle under a rather substantial frame.

First Acquaintance The cliché of the road to success being long and hard is nowhere truer than here, when the partnership is first opened between horse and rider. So, if you are very young, I would say, 'Arm yourself with patience'; if you are a little older, 'Never let patience slip'. Training for showing – whether in dressage, jumping, or eventing – is but the process of forming, improving and maintaining a loyal, unwavering partnership for better or for worse.

At the formation stage do not be over-anxious for progress. Use the first week or so to become mutually acquainted. Here you have a great advantage over the horse. You may feel a bit strange on his back but this is a purely mechanical problem and is easily overcome in a few days. For him, on the other hand, everything is new and strange. As a result of his move his appetite and digestion may be a little affected and he may appear to be restless or jittery in his box, which won't help him to get a good night's sleep. He is tense and nervous when you want to ride him, not in anticipation of having you on his back, but following a bad day and night in the box. It may be that he will brood over his former stables, his past companions or his old groom, and when you ride him you may feel let down because he moved so much better when you tried him at his home stables. But give him time and let your behaviour, your gestures, your voice, your care of him, all encourage him to put his trust in you. So long as he is not visibly glad to see you in the morning and does not leave his box with a certain joyfulness, do not ask him for anything. Just go hacking, day after day, long outings at slow gaits, allowing the utmost freedom of the neck, though never losing contact with the mouth.

The main purpose of these hacks is to deepen the relationship between the two of you and they are not a waste of time. It will take two or three weeks, sometimes longer, before you can truly begin to work; but the hacks will always go on. By and by they will take on the name of WORK, as opposed to LESSONS, which take place in the school or arena. There must be no confusion about this. *Work* is a physical health exercise and keeps keenness intact or if necessary improves it. It is protracted but never overtaxing. *Lessons*, on the other hand, teach and improve the movements. They are short, never monotonous and are always broken by brief rest periods.

Though quite distinct, work and lessons are obviously related and therefore are interdependent. So each must be given with due regard for what happens in the other. If, for example, your horse lacks energy or keenness, you will quite naturally play down the lessons for a while and emphasize the outdoor work, it being normal for a rather unambitious horse to be less eager to deliver up his impulsive forces between four walls. Conversely, if he is the sort who is distracted at the drop of a pin, inattentive to orders, or a little too dashing for your taste and comfort, you should put rather more stress on the indoor lessons. It is up to you to know him sufficiently to apply the right means for his education.

Proof of success is a horse equally keen, disciplined and attentive both indoors and outdoors.

Chapter 2

RIDING IN TUNE

We have discussed what we expect of our horse, and it is now time to consider what he expects of us in school and arena. First of all, leadership, knowing what we want and knowing how to convey our will to him. It is not enough to know the music, we must play it for him in key and without hitting the wrong notes because we have become wrongly positioned in relation to our 'keyboard', or because a jolt unhinges us or keeps us from measuring our impact.

This brings us to the POSITION in the saddle. A good one adds to the grace of the whole picture but its function is far more than that. A good position gives precision, effectiveness and discretion to the aids. Dressage tests demand proof that horse and rider have reached a level of training where they can execute a well-defined sequence of certain movements in close succession, not only without effort, but with ease. To do so, we must be able to change our aids swiftly without impairing the horse's balance and without the motions in themselves becoming obvious.

The horse's centre of gravity runs along a vertical line going through the withers, so that the closer you sit to it (i.e. to the pommel of your saddle), the less you will feel the movement of the gaits and the easier it is to be with your horse. Do not stiffen up or let yourself go but hold yourself up

9

straight, shoulders squared, head erect and well out of your shoulders. Let your arms drop naturally along your body, elbows bent, wrists held up in prolongation of the forearms, fingers closed over the reins, thumbs uppermost, fingernails face to face. Thighs, legs, toes drop normally by their own weight. The tread of the stirrup should be in a line with your ankle when your feet are out of the irons and allowed to go limp. When the foot is placed in the iron the toe must point upwards. You are sitting properly when an imaginary line passes from ears over shoulders, over hips, to heels.

This long explanation is as basically necessary to equitation as the multiplication table is for mathematics, and before you can go any farther it must have become the only natural and comfortable way of sitting for you. Now let us look at the details.

If you carry your HEAD properly (high), looking in the direction you are taking, your overall position can hardly be all bad and changes of direction, also, are made easier. If you lower your head looking at your hands, everything goes wrong: the shoulders slump, the back hunches, the hands recede to your stomach, your seat moves towards the cantle, your legs advance and the changes of direction lose precision, the horse seeming to 'drift' rather than to move with precision.

As to the SEAT itself, you do not sit in the saddle as you would on a chair. Your buttocks must be pushed forward under you; if you sit as though on a chair you are poised on the crutch. Sitting properly, you have good adherence and can use your seat as a third aid to complement the hands and legs.

The LOINS are for the rider what the shock absorber is for a motor-car. If you stiffen them they cannot play their part and you will bounce at trot and canter. The small of the back must play freely in all directions if you want your seat to remain in place and go with your horse, and feel what is going on underneath you. If we speak of the 'aid' of the seat, rather than that of loins or back, it is because it is your seat which acts in contact with the horse, not your back, the action of which is but a consequence of that made by the seat. It is your seat which encourages, promotes, accompanies or opposes the movements of the horse. In other words, the role of the loins is subordinate to that of the seat, not vice versa.

As to the LEGS, one does not stick on by pressing knees in to the saddle, but through suppleness. The legs must be in close contact with the horse but they must not cling to him. The more points of contact you have with your horse the closer you are to him, and the closer you are the more contact you will have. So you want to keep your whole leg, particularly the lower part, in contact with the flank but without squeezing. If you press with your knee the lower part of the leg cannot help but shoot outward and lose steadiness. If your legs do not keep this permanent gentle contact they will, when used as aids, necessarily act by fits and starts, and any subtle nuance in their use becomes impossible. Your horse will not be in the channel of the aids but will be able to escape your control; perhaps only by just a little, but a little is too much.

The TOES are raised, mark my words, the heels are not lowered. To all appearances, but it is only to appearances, the result is the same. When the toes are dropped naturally so that the stirrup tread is at ankle height and you slip your foot into the stirrup, it is your toes which are raised, not your heel that is lowered. Your heel remains where it was, that is, somewhat below the stirrup tread. 'Heels down' is a consequence, not an end in itself. If, hearing this command, you push them down, you stiffen the thigh and leg muscles and contract the knee and ankle joints which makes it hard for you to use your legs efficiently. Raising your toes, tightens a single muscle in front of the leg, between knee and ankle, which does not hamper their freedom of movement.

Chapter 3

UNDERSTANDING THE AIDS

We have analysed why only the classical position can provide a stable base for effective and precise use of the aids – aids which are discreet whilst being unmistakable in their clarity.

Hands and legs are our chief aids, the combination being completed by that of the seat.

Speaking of legs, we mean calves, heels and, if need be, spurs, the ultimate spokesmen for the legs. The spurs have their place on the training ground where they are used to make the horse sensitive to, and respectful of, our legs, making him respond by producing the desired movement or by giving greater impulsion. Their use is delicate at all times, and on the day we enter the arena we had better keep them strictly decorative. The whip is officially banned from the dressage arena, but it is used during early training and then again during advanced work, in hand. In our kind of work we may say, as they do at Saumur, that 'legs are for the horseman, whips for the handicapped'.

Both hands and legs operate by *acting, resisting* or *yielding*. The impulsion generated by the legs is received by the hands which control, regulate and filter it, just as though the horse were a steam boiler, the legs being the fuel and the hands the safety valve.

The hands – controlling this impulsion by regulating speed and giving direction – act by varying finger pressures and there is no need for them to remain other than still. Since the reins pass underneath the fifth finger and come out between thumb and index, their tension is changed and controlled by the opening or closing of the last three fingers. Using these fingers separately or in combination is like 'playing' an instrument which the thumb and index finger have 'tuned' when they closed at a chosen point on the reins. There are infinite nuances in changing rein tension. Let the little finger yield on its own for example, then try two fingers and then yield with all of them. Learning to play these nuances is learning to ride, learning to play them subtly is becoming a proficient rider. Wherever you may stand between these points there is no need to move your hands when riding a reasonably trained horse.

The hands *act* when they slow down the pace, or check it to a lower one, as from canter to trot. They act, also, to bring the horse to halt, to ask a rein back or to change direction. The hands *resist* by fixing themselves at a given spot *like a wall*, a fact which makes them very potent, yet less irritating to the horse than would be a live and moving force. They *yield* when the fingers slacken to decrease rein tension and they follow the movements of neck and head. But they can do nothing unless they do it on an 'adjusted' rein, that is, one that is taut and even and through which the contact with the mouth is being channelled.

We might say that the legs, in the same way, must be 'adjusted'. In other words, they must be in permanent contact with the flanks, which is a contact as infinitely variable as that of the hands with the mouth, and is greatly dependent on the sensibility of the horse and the tact of the rider.

The legs, like the hands, can as I said before, act, resist or yield. They act simultaneously and together, to increase impulsion or speed or to pass to a stronger gait and they act in the same way to obtain the engagement of the hind legs. The single leg acts to shift the haunches one way or another. The legs resist, and this also is like a wall, to oppose a movement of the horse's initiative, such as an unwanted shift of haunches. They yield by relaxing or by ceasing to act or to resist, but always they keep a light contact and are ready to intervene if necessary.

Here I would put an end to the nonsense we hear all too often about owning a horse 'too sensitive for contact with the legs', one who goes wild at their mere approach. This same 'sensitive child' is expected to accept on his back a weight which is not always as steady as it might be and which is far more keenly felt than the light contact of legs, and he must also put up with hands acting on his mouth, not always tenderly, by means of a piece of steel. Of course, he will accept the legs providing his rider can apply them steadily and in a controlled fashion.

Take a young horse, barely backed and not having felt the legs at all. Spread your legs from knees to heels so as to prevent even the faintest contact, then approach his flanks with both simultaneously, applying pressure very gradually with equal intensity once the legs are touching the flanks. If the pressure is coming on gradually, continuously, smoothly, nine out of ten horses won't move.

Hence the horse does accept unambiguous contact with the legs just so long as they do not shift about. Pressure, after all, does not automatically entail forward movement and the various forms of leg action have no natural significance to the horse, who has to be taught their meaning. So ride with your legs in contact, and if the horse will not accept this go back and teach him to accept the legs as he was taught to accept the bit and body weight before you undertake anything more.

The Aids: How? 'Now bring back your right leg,' or, 'At this point, the rider should act with his left hand. . . .' Teachers frequently speak or write in this way about the WHICH, WHEN and WHERE of the aids but their pupils do not always achieve the proper results because they have not learnt HOW these aids should be applied. Yet it is only, in reality, a matter of mastering certain basic skills; believe me, it is nothing to do with magic.

Hand action, for example, depends largely on shoulders and arms, because the reins extend from the horse's mouth along your arms all the way up to your shoulders. The contractions of your shoulders, therefore, run down along your arms and reins, reverberating in the horse's mouth. You must, therefore, learn to relax the shoulders and to *keep* them relaxed, holding your elbows close to your body, your arms dropping naturally from shoulders to elbows, if the rein tension is not to change constantly. You will not notice these changes in tension but the horse will, and he will react accordingly.

Rigidity, or instability, in these parts of the body must be eliminated because they interfere with your hands' first duty which, whether they are acting, resisting or yielding, is to develop, improve and safeguard a soft mouth. The disappearance of this quality in the mouth instantly affects the horse's general behaviour and his performance of movements and gaits. What is more, it shows. More often than not a hard mouth is due to a lack of softness in our hands – and if we want to be sure of never pulling, we must not retract them at any time. Rather increases in rein tension must be made solely by finger pressures, reinforced, if necessary, by resisting shoulders. Whatever the resistance we make with our hands must be strictly commensurate with that put up by the horse and it must cease *instantly* the moment he yields. '*A main galante, bouche galante*' – gallant mouth to gallant hand!

Leg action, while as delicate and finely shaded as that of the hands, is much less natural to the horse, who must be trained to understand it. It should take the form of brief, recurrent taps, ranging from weak to strong – mere pulsations, in fact, of the calves at the bottom of the scale, spur attacks at the top, both resembling the staccato of the hammer of an electric bell, not the continuous action of the pneumatic drill.

The effectiveness of the leg in obtaining the forward movement, its main function, depends on the horse's sensibility and generosity, and on his training and your own. That is, you must have learnt how to make proper use of your legs. The principal problem of the forward movement, however, is psychological. The horse must be made to understand from the beginning that at the quiet *prompting of the legs* he must move forward, an awareness which must eventually be sharpened to the point where he advances at the mere *permission of the hands*, the legs remaining, so to speak, in reserve.

At first we can go so far as to sacrifice the otherwise essential contact with the mouth, and, if reaction to the initial request of the legs is not forthcoming with due promptness, let progressively stronger action follow on the spot in the way of taps with the calves, the heels, and then, if need be, the spurs or even the whip. It is clearly pointless, and even dangerous, to set the horse on the bit *before* the forward movement has become truly automatic for the reason that hand and bit at one end combining with ineffective leg action at the other is only likely to cause restiveness in the animal.

The efficiency of the action of the single leg, shifting the haunches, is a matter of timing rather than degree. In a half-turn on the forehand, for example, you cannot expect your horse to move his near hind, for instance, at the prompting of your left leg if you apply it at the very moment when he is carrying his weight on that particular limb. If, on the other hand, your leg acts at the moment when the horse's off-hind is carrying his weight and his near-hind is therefore free, then the crossing of the legs will be made easy for him. The same is true, of course, when working on two tracks.

Nevertheless, you must also remember that the action of the leg to shift the haunches is different from its action when asking for forward movement. In the first instance the leg acts to the rear, in the second from rear to front. Both these movements should in time be minimal and eventually invisible though they must always be entirely obvious to the horse.

These are movements which must be learned, so do not hesitate to exaggerate them at first by spreading your legs and then, for the forward movement, taking them back a little in order to bring them forward again to their normal place under an increase of pressure which gives the movement a somewhat rounded character. The same thing, in reverse, is carried out when the leg asks for a shift of the haunches. But remember that the thighs and knees remain in place, they should never take part in the action of the lower leg.

Of the seat we may expect no more at this point than that it should be supple enough to remain with our horse in movement and balance, the flexibility of the small of the back keeping us from bumping in the saddle. In other words, for the time being, we look upon it as a passive aid.

What we can do, though, by looking where we are going, whether on straight lines or curves, is to weight, automatically, the saddle in the right place at the right moment, thus making sure that we do not disturb the horse's balance. This is done by slightly advancing the outside shoulder on a curves so that the body faces the direction in which we are travelling. The right shoulder, for example, would be advanced when circling to the left and vice-versa.

This transference of weight, putting more emphasis on one buttock than the other, is only one of two forms of intervention by the seat. There is also the more accentuated movement made to push the horse on in his current gait, or a lesser body movement allowing the pace to remain unaltered. Further by these means we can oppose an unwanted initiative on the part of the horse.

We can, as an example, without changing the position of the upper body, make one buttock bear more weight than the other, a very keenly felt difference for the horse, since the weight added to one side is taken off the other.

Our normal movement when staying with the horse at the canter may be exaggerated in order to drive him on, or it may be diminished when the sole aim is to remain at the current gait. Then, so that we shall not counteract the movement of the rein back, we will allow our seat to follow the movement felt, very lightly; whereas at the halt, our seat is blocked to keep the hind legs engaged.

But before you can feel you must learn, and before you can learn you must feel, and for some time this will be your problem should you want to use the seat as an 'active aid'.

Independent but in Concert In reviewing how our hands and legs can act, resist or yield we have been looking at the positive side of the question of aids, on the premise that the negative has been resolved. Alas, this is not always the case. As yet it is unlikely that we will have reached the stage where our hands and legs are under such perfect control that they can be used accurately and precisely without being upset by the horse's reactions. Our quest for this control is complicated by the fact that it is extremely difficult to move a particular hand or leg without it affecting the other limbs. If you try to make a few asymmetric movements with your arms you will realize how hard it is. When you have to think about your legs, too, it is even more difficult and, not surprisingly, the difficulty increases when you are on a horse and your legs are expected to make different and independent movements.

This is why we should not for the moment attempt to use extremely refined or complicated aids. We are incapable of doing so, even if we have the most complete theoretical knowledge, for the simple reason that our limbs cannot translate into physical action the theory absorbed by our brains. Our best plan, from now and all the way to the top, is to improve the functioning of our aids up to perfection on the current plane, and only after that has been achieved to move on to the one above. THE INDEPENDENCE OF THE AIDS is contingent on the seat, without which we cannot stay 'with' our horse. Our seat must be sufficiently supple and pliable to allow us to remain relaxed enough to operate the aids smoothly. A good seat, however, is not sufficient, unless accompanied by steadiness which, conversely, is unthinkable without a good seat. Only if we are steady in the saddle will we avoid making unnecessary and, perhaps, harmful movements. But steadiness is not synonymous with immobility; we are steady in relation to our moving horse. Steadiness in equestrian terms is not a static quality.

Our aids must, like a football team, work 'independently but in concert', so if one of the keys to equitation, as we already know, is the good balance of the horse, the other is good CO-ORDINATION OF THE AIDS. Gaspar de Saunier told his contemporaries that he overheard a French nobleman ask the great eighteenth-century master, Duplessis, to teach his son, 'not to be an *écuyer*, just to co-ordinate his hands and legs with what he had in mind', then he quoted the master's reply, that this had been the object of his own search 'for these past sixty years' and that he was still searching for it.

After just a few months' riding, every movement will require the participation of both legs and both hands. Each leg has a well-defined assignment of its own which is quite distinct from its partner, and the same is true of the hands, one of which is always either permitting or reinforcing the action of the other. At first we only try to keep legs and hands from making the worst mistakes, then we go through a transitional period where these bad reflexes are no longer so much of a problem but where applying the aids correctly demands some thought, which usually results in the aids being applied a little late. Eventually it is the good habits we have learnt that predominate, but, of course, there is still, as always, room for improvement.

Until well into the second phase most riders tend to make too much use of their hands and too little of their legs, though the role of the hands is quite clearly subsidiary to the action of the legs. Nevertheless, since both are equally necessary, neither should predominate to the exclusion of the other but should operate in proper co-ordination.

Doubtless, the instructor's explanations will be helpful in teaching us to use our hands and legs in such a way and sequence as to obtain a specific movement. But this help can only be given preparatory to the actual movement, since once we are in motion the aids must move more swiftly than he can voice his advice. For there is just one right, precisely timed, instant to act, and the same aids applied either before or after that split-second of truth will, at best, be ineffective. At the worst they can run counter to the horse's action and become downright negative. Another thing the teacher cannot indicate, and this is the great problem, is the strength of intensity of the aids at any particular moment or for any particular movement. He cannot do so because it is not he but the ever-changing horse who dictates from one moment to the next the intensity of the aid we must apply. Finally, there is the feel of the horse. Only the rider can sense its impulsion, balance or lightness at any given moment, and only he can sense incipient resistance. If a resistance reaches the proportions of being noticeable, then, certainly, the instructor can help, but the slight, incipient resistance can only be detected by the rider.

Give and Take There are several terms used to classify the aids. We use the words *natural* and *artificial* to distinguish between hands and legs and whip and spurs; we say *upper* and *lower,* meaning hands and legs, and we also talk about *active* and *passive* aids, those that either act, resist, yield or limit. Then there are the *lateral* and *diagonal* aids, when either hand and leg on the same side act, or when they do so on opposite sides. We will all be familiar with these terms, but really only two apply in practice: the active and passive and the lateral and diagonal aids.

The concept of active and passive aids is particularly interesting, because so few riders are aware of what it implies, and even the enlightened ones do not always apply their knowledge. The main implication is that one must know how to give, which few seem able to do, although everybody, somehow, knows how to take.

Every time a hand acts, the more so if both do, this action may be compared to that of a brake. Consequently, it provokes a slowing down. The decrease in pace may not be immediately evident nor a very pronounced one, but at least morally the horse senses an opposition to the former movement. If the hand action is wrong, he will fight it, more or less promptly, in one way or another. Either he will withdraw his impulsive forces or he will pull in order to escape. In any case, we shall be no longer in a position to control him correctly and a struggle will ensue. The horse will stiffen up and contract himself, and so most likely will we. It is a vicious circle. If he balks, and we are no longer raw beginners, we use our legs to drive him 'onto the hand'; and many instructors, no longer raw beginners either, will let it go at shouting 'Legs, legs!' – which is far from sensible. Beware of slogans used out of context – they are dangerous things.

If the horse balks because he fears a hand too hard for the sensitivity of his mouth we shall not overcome the difficulty by using our legs to push him even more energetically onto this ignorant hand. On the contrary, we shall only increase his exasperation. In short, we must know when and how to use our legs, and, furthermore, with what intensity they can be used in relation to our hand.

If our hands are 'intelligent', and we know how to make them so acceptable to the horse that he trusts them, the legs have a minimal part to play. If they are not and tend to provoke a struggle each time they come into use then the legs must be extraordinarily strong to make the horse accept contact with the bit. Even if this can be done the effect is one of force-cum-resistance and will be rightly penalized in a dressage test.

Undoubtedly, the part played by the legs is important, since it is they which create the forward movement without which riding becomes impossible. In the case of beginners, who invariably ride more with their hands than their legs, the instructor's slogan 'Legs, always the legs, and again the legs', is used in the correct context. In this instance the teacher is trying to inculcate the idea of forward movement into his pupils just as the trainer does with his horse.

There comes, however, a time when both horse and rider must understand more subtle implications; when the effect our legs have on the horse becomes more moral than physical. The trainer, when he works his horse in hand, or on the lunge line, is not pinching him between his legs and yet he obtains by a grazing with the whip or a clicking of the tongue the most perfectly free forward movement. Once he has inculcated into the horse the almost obsessive urge to advance at the faintest signal, it is up to the rider to use his knowledgeable, educated hands to permit and encourage this 'fixed idea' to materialize.

Let us now take a look at some concrete cases and the bearing all this has on them. The hands yield when both legs act to create or augment impulsion (forward movement). The legs, on the contrary, yield when the hands act in order to slow down or halt the forward progression. One hand yields when the other acts to change direction or bend the horse; one leg yields when the other acts to shift the haunches.

These are truisms, for otherwise the aids would contradict each other. And yet, from the beginning we seem to run up against difficulties by failing *to yield before we act*. As an example, when we want our horse to walk out from the halt, our hands must yield *before* our legs act.

This kind of co-ordination of aids is simple; it does not require great experience, only a little forethought. But soon co-ordination must become more refined, more precise, and, above all, more complex. There is a great deal of food for thought in the fact that from the very moment the rider 'intervenes' the management of the horse requires the use of his two hands and legs for any correct movement, and that his intervention begins the moment he sits down in the saddle.

Let me give you a little immediate food for thought by asking you to ride an imaginary left circle. Before doing so you will need some reserve impulsion, because by leaving the track and being ignorant of the direction he will be made to take, the horse will tend to slow down. Almost instantaneously your weight must enter into action by a slight advance of the right shoulder to keep you facing in this direction. Slightly forward of its normal place, your left leg, around which the horse will bend, attends to the impulsion. Slightly back, the right leg keeps the haunches from escaping to the right and makes them stay on the track you have chosen. The left hand flexes the neck just sufficiently to bend the whole horse in accordance with the circle's curvature and at the same time keeps the direction, while the right must yield at the start to let the left inflect the neck and must then resist to reinforce the action of the left hand and perhaps even help it keep direction by using a counter-rein. On top of everything else, both hands must unceasingly control the speed, regulate the impulsion, make sure the jaw remains relaxed and attend to the balance.

This is a random example of the problems involved in the co-ordination of the aids, and if the beginning-to-average rider tries to put it into effect in all its details he will fumble and fail and his horse along with him. Even if the average-to-proficient rider applies it correctly to the last aid, his horse, if not itself sufficiently trained, will still make a mess of it. Thus both horse and rider must have followed an adequate progression and have arrived at an adequate level of training before venturing anywhere near a dressage arena.

Chapter 4

THE RIDER AS TRAINER AND THE FIRST COMMANDMENT

We have discussed the active and passive aids which are of particular interest in both the simplest form of riding and the highest reaches of dressage. In looking now at the *lateral* and *diagonal* aids, we shall be slipping a little way into the territory of training.

I told you at the start that I was providing you with a 'trained horse', addressing you as a rider, not a trainer. But what is commonly called 'the training period' is, in reality, a period during which the horse has learned just as much as his particular trainer intended to teach him, and the sum total of his attainment will depend on what level his trainer originally had in mind. The horse may, therefore, be trained to quite a high degree or, on the other hand and with a different trainer, still be almost green.

Here we suppose that your horse has been trained to the point where you can both take the final step towards the dressage arena; but if you think you can be just a user of a trained horse (that is, go for a ride on one without the slightest intention of furthering his training) you will be disappointed. No matter how 'neutral' you may be you will not improve him, and you will probably finish up by ruining your mount. Since a horse is not a machine which can be regulated by a switch to a certain unchangeable level of efficiency we must touch on training matters even here.

Now, one of the schooling means are the lateral aids which should, whenever possible, be given preference in training. Even movements requiring the diagonal aids should, regardless of what this may do to the horse's position, first be worked on by lateral aids. The horse understands the lateral aids better and yields more naturally to them, while the constricting diagonal aids are liable to occasion struggle and delay.

Take the half-turn on the forehand, which requires the diagonal aids: on a right turn, action of the right leg (active aid) and the left counter-rein (passive aid), to keep the shoulders from shifting left. Though it is only in this way that the movement can be performed properly, we should begin by using the lateral aids on the right: i.e. right leg and hand. The horse will slightly shift his shoulders to the left but will yield better to the action of the right leg by shifting his haunches to the left, and this is capital. Moreover, and above all, the forward movement won't be affected by his being caught between right leg and left hand. Once he has understood the mechanics of the new movement, we may little by little go over to the diagonal aids.

The same is true for the departures at the canter. Before going on to the diagonal aids, we begin by using the outside lateral aids, once more disregarding the effect it has on the horse's position.

What matters in riding, even beyond training, is to make oneself understood by one's horse, and the simpler and clearer our requests the more easily will they be carried out by the horse.

The logical sequence from simple to complex is only part of what is called 'methodical procedure'. Another part is the setting aside while working on a new movement (however prepared the horse may be for it) all that is extraneous to it, so as to lay full stress on essentials and not to muddle up our aids.

'Never chase more than one hare at a time,' be clear in your mind as to the primary purpose of each lesson, and of the means by which you plan to pursue it, and base the next lesson's programme on its results. Ask for whatever is 'new' at the end of the lesson so that the slightest obedience can be rewarded by sending your horse instantly back to the stables.

Rewards, and incidentally punishments, are of course particularly meaningful in training and though used less and more moderately in time, they never lose their importance. Reward should occur more frequently than punishment; for if we are patient, and do not ask for too much, we are naturally called upon to reward more often than to punish, while if we keep our horse too long under subjection we are bound to drive him to rebellion. This revolt is not always immediately apparent, at least not to the inexperienced who do not feel or the careless who do not want to feel. By the time it becomes overt, however, we may be unable to cope with it in a normal way and feel compelled to have recourse to punishment. Think how much simpler it would have been after ten minutes of attentive work or at the improved performance of a movement to reward by giving a few minutes' rest. Human nature tends to take for granted whatever is right and dwells only on what is wrong; and yet horsemanship, like life-manship, gains immeasurably by a timely show of appreciation. Effort without recognition in both fields leads to apathy or revolt.

Punishment is much more delicate to administer, because, while the very motivation for reward tends to put us into a calm, good-natured frame of mind, punishment tends to be given in a state of incipient anger or impatience. And yet, more than anything else, it requires calm and perfect self-control. It must be given commensurate with the fault committed and a bare few seconds later equanimity must reign as before. The matter is further complicated by the fact that, while reward follows obedience, incipient or fully materialized, punishment often follows something that has not materialized. The horse may have failed to obey because he does not understand or because he is physically incapable. Punishment in such cases is out of place and very harmful because horses, like children, are especially sensitive to injustice and, having a great memory, resent the rider who administers punishment indiscriminately. Particular caution is necessary with young horses, where we must learn to distinguish between a buck, for instance, given out of malice or from sheer *joie de vivre*.

One thing is true for both reward and punishment; each must follow instantly the act which prompted them, and the wise trainer is the one who 'requests often, is satisfied with little, rewards a great deal'.

It is not by chance that I have concluded this first general discussion of the aids with a few pointers on method and psychology. If the effect of our aids is physically contingent on our seat and position, morally it is contingent on the horse's state of mind and our own – his preparedness and receptivity, our discipline and patience. Where all this is present calm exists, and calm is the point of departure, the only one, for action.

The First Commandment The catechism of riding is short: 'calm, forward and straight'. These three commandments apply equally to horse and rider. Let us consider the first of this trinity.

Calm must always be present, not only when things are going well but when everything goes wrong. Most particularly, it must be present in the rider at the moment of punishment.

We know that calm is as communicable as nervousness, and that the horse, extremely impressionable animal that he is, detects in his rider the faintest wavering. Whenever we feel in danger of losing our calm we had better give the horse a rest for as long as it takes us to recover it. A certain firm believer in 'the blessings of the timely cigarette', whom I knew, and himself a non-smoker, used to carry a packet for exasperated pupils during difficult lessons. At any rate, if ever we lose our calm and cannot promptly regain it, we had better leave the school and go for a hack, or else alight and return the horse to the stables. It won't be wasted time; at worse no progress is made that day, but at least we have made no retrograde steps in our relationship with our horse.

If a calm outlook on the part of the horse is based upon his trust in his rider it follows that trust can only come about in an atmosphere of calm. This is so important that we should understand how a horse can acquire calm, develop it and even lose it.

To start with let us be quite sure that we do not, as many do, confuse a high-strung with a high-bred horse. The highly-strung is really a compulsive extrovert, the high-bred is a horse rich in physical, moral and mental qualities. Despite exceptions, it may be said that the Thoroughbred has a quicker understanding than a part-bred horse and that the quality of his tissues, bones and tendons tend to be superior. Also, he is 'keen' and capable of producing great effort long after he has grown physically tired, because of the 'courage' with which he is so amply endowed.

Even among these horses we will find extroverts, introverts, and normally constituted characters. The highly-strung horse reacts strongly to all or most sensory perceptions. He has, indeed, a moral and/or a physical vulnerability which can be expressed to a pathological degree. This state, which would be called 'neurotic' in the human, is called 'crazy' or 'dangerous' when it occurs in the horse. We should no more trust or set our hopes in a crazy animal partner than we would in a neurotic human. But we have chosen a normal horse, as well balanced in body and mind as we think ourselves to be. But what about the stable yard atmosphere? Is our groom as calmly firm and firmly calm as we are? Or is he, without meaning any harm, frightening the daylights out of our perhaps young, certainly, at first, somewhat bewildered animal by loud guffaws and violent motions? Calm does not mean dull monotony, nor is it necessary to entertain our horse continually, but it is essential that he should be kept from growing bored. Too many horses when off work are stowed away in a dark corner with nothing to see but a bare piece of wall, and here begins boredom which ends in mental, emotional and even physical sluggishness. Life in the stables should go along calmly but that does not exclude the horse from taking an interest in life. Playing a radio, if it is not up too loud, is a simple antidote to boredom and is appreciated by horses.

During work, however, all distractions are to be avoided, the horse's undivided attention must then be focused on his rider, or else the better part of what we are so painstakingly trying to instil will be lost on him. The ideal place for schooling is a covered school, where the horse can be immune to distractions and where we can work whatever the weather outside.

By taking sensible precautions to ensure that our horse is neither bored nor frightened in his stable and by never exceeding his capacity for concentration by working for too long at a time without rests all should go well, and calm will be preserved in both horse and rider.

Chapter 5

THE HORSE TURNS BY
BOTH ENDS

At this point we should be sure of our aims and of our horse (and he sure of us). Also, we should by now be sure of our position and aids and of at least the first commandment of the riding catechism, absolute calm. This is not the first commandment because it is the most important of the three, but because until calm is complete we cannot begin any constructive work on the other two or, in fact, on anything else.

Assuming that we have reached this point we can now begin studying the different movements, starting with the one which is an integral part of nearly all of them, the change of direction.

One tends to forget that the horse may turn in three different ways. He does so by his body pivoting around the hind legs or around the forelegs or by both ends at once, all four legs shifting as he turns around a vertical axis located at the girth.

At liberty he does the latter because it is easiest for him. The first (half-turn-on-the-haunches type) he will do on rare occasions, usually when he is frightened and wants to change direction abruptly and almost on the spot. The second (turning solely around the forehand) he can safely be said never to do of his own volition.

And yet this half-turn on the forehand is, if we want to make his haunches light, our first method of teaching him to yield to the single leg.

Why is this lightness of the haunches so important? Because the great and principal seat of the *resistances* is in the haunches, where the 'engine' is. Even when we find a lack of lightness at the front end it often has its origins in the haunches and so it is to them that we must return, making them shift laterally, swinging them from leg to leg, and then, quite often, the resistance in the forehand will vanish by itself.

Moreover, *changes of direction*, which positioning of the neck can only indicate, are actually imposed by the positioning of the haunches. To turn left, for example, your left rein bends your horse's neck left and makes him look to the left as well. But suppose he throws his haunches also to the left? He will be going to the right because whenever front and back end are in conflict the back end wins.

Why this happens is not hard to understand. Because head and neck can move independently of the rest of the body they are not sufficiently related to it to determine the direction of the shoulders. This movement is dictated by the haunches which are connected to the trunk. So let it be well understood that changes of direction are *prepared by positioning the haunches and then carried out with the head in the lead.* Count d'Aure used to say that one must pre-position the haunches as a sailor would his rudder in determining a change of course. This principle, far from applying only to young riders and/or horses, remains valid all the way to the Grand Prix Dressage Test.

In changes of direction initiated by the forehand, lightness, the great fetish of dressage, is lost, because the haunches keep driving in the original direction while the shoulders are taking another course. The haunches then form a sort of buttress, obstructing change and, no matter how light the horse had seemed in walking straight ahead, a more or less pronounced resistance appears as he starts into the change. The 'harmony of the forces' is lost if we do not *pre-position the seat of impulsion for the change of direction and have the head and neck position instantly adjusted to it.*

How this lateral mobility of the haunches should be obtained will become clear in the half-turn on the forehand, which we shall discuss in detail. It is only when we are able to shift the haunches easily that we will be able to hold them in place for the half-turn on the haunches, correct circles, voltes, serpentines and other movements requiring the horse to move on curves.

The Half-turn on the Forehand A half-turn on the forehand is carried out on the spot, one foreleg serving as a pivot (the off-fore when the haunches are driven to the left, the near-fore when driven to the right). All four limbs must be mobile, including the pivot leg, which, though it moves neither forward nor sideways, must lift and touch down on the spot whenever its turn in the four-time beat of the walk comes up.

To make sure of getting in the whole progression we shall asssume that the horse is not yet accustomed to the single leg, the instrument we use (acting by itself behind its normal place) to shift the haunches or to oppose any unwanted move-ment on their part.

Our first aim is to teach him to cross his hind legs so that THE CROSSING LIMB PASSES IN FRONT OF THE CROSSED LIMB. To do this the horse *must* be allowed to advance.

Let us deal with a concrete example. We want to obtain a left half-turn on the forehand, where the haunches are driven

35

from right to left around the off shoulder. Now if you will stop to re-read and analyse this sentence the directions to follow will be clear. Whenever you want to apply them to the right half-turn, you just reverse the words *right* and *left*.

So now to work on the *left half-turn* which we shall do, first, on foot, to make it easier for both the horse and ourselves. We stand by his head on the off-side facing the croup, then take a pace or two backwards inviting him to advance with us by clicks of the tongue and sharp but not rough touches on the off-flank with a rather long whip held in the left hand. Both reins are held about four inches from the mouth in the right hand.

As soon as easy compliance is obtained in moving straight ahead – that is, when a couple of clicks without benefit of whip have repeatedly prompted the horse to walk out from the halt– we ask, again with the help of the whip, for a slight left shift of the haunches. He will better understand us if we draw his head a little to the right (towards us) and slow down the walk by a faint opposition of our right hand but WITHOUT EVER LETTING HIM STOP.

No sooner has he given us a couple of forward steps, crossing his hind legs, than we let him rest a while and tell him by a pat that, though his movement was but a hint of things to come, he is headed in the right direction.

We finish up by reversing the aids, doing the same exercise in the opposite direction with the haunches now shifting from left to right, and at that point we bring the day's lesson to an end. Remember that all new things should come at the conclusion of the lesson so that an instant return to the stables can follow a satisfactory performance. We do this not only because the horse deserves a reward but because in this way the horse retains in his mind a sharp impression of the new movement.

The next step is to repeat the lesson in the saddle, combining the action of our right leg (quite far back to begin with) with that of the whip, applying both just where the latter was used during the work on foot. As before, we always work *going forward*, always slowing down from an active walk before prompting the lateral shift of the haunches. Eventually the horse will yield to the sole action of the right leg.

I hardly need to mention that at each of these stages the work is done on both sides, with more emphasis being placed on the side to which the horse has more difficulty in making the movement. Thus the horse will be made equally light to either hand. Once this point is reached we can think about improving the movement and begin the half-turn on the forehand which is also called 'half-pirouette in reverse.'

For this purpose we use *reversed half-voltes*, the same basic figure as the half-volte, but, as the name implies, ridden in reverse. Instead of leaving the track by the half-circle and regaining it by the oblique track to the wall, as in the half-volte, we leave the track on the oblique line and regain it by riding the half-circle. (Fig. I).

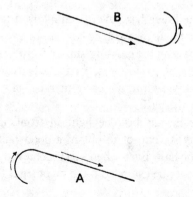

Fig. 1 (A) Half volte and (B) Reversed half volte.

Keeping the example of the left half-turn on the forehand in mind, we start on the left rein and first ride an ordinary reversed half-volte in which the hind-legs strictly follow the fore-legs and the half circle leading back to the track has an 18 ft. diameter. Then we start again but this time, at the end of the oblique and before starting into the half-circle which will bring us back to the track, we slow down the walk and simultaneously let our right leg act backwards in an effort to obtain a shift of the haunches to the left. By doing so we are driving the hind legs outside the track made by the fore-legs.

We support the backward motion of our right leg by an equal advance of the left and we do not look at the leg which shifts the haunches. If we were to look to the right we would automatically be lightening the near-side of the horse and burdening the off-side. What we should be doing is precisely the opposite; our weight should be placed, of course, on the side to which the haunches are shifting.

By tightening the reversed half-volte little by little and making the half-circle gradually smaller, we reach the stage where we are executing a half-turn on the forehand at the walk.

Because the horse has never been allowed to stop, always being made to move forward, he has had to cross his hind legs properly by passing the crossing limb in front of the other and, as an added bonus, his forelegs, particularly the pivot leg, have remained mobile within a clearly marked gait of four-time, however slow the pace.

Only after he has become light in front, and thus well balanced, may we expect to obtain a good half-turn on the forehand at the halt. Even when this is achieved, however, the halt should never be extended if the pivot leg is to maintain its mobility.

The diagonal aids for the left half-turn on the forehand

(around the off-shoulder) are as follows: slow down the walk; right leg back to demand shift of the haunches to the left (active aid); left counter-rein to keep the shoulders in place and avoid their shifting to the left; weight on the left buttock without impairing the straightness of the upper body; left leg at the girth to maintain impulsion. Finally, go again into the walk as soon as the half-turn has been fully executed.

Obviously, in acquainting our horse with the use of these aids we once more follow a progression. At first we only act with the leg which shifts the haunches (the right in our example); then we use a direct rein of opposition on the same side as the acting leg in order to block some of the shoulders' forward movement. This direct rein of opposition, also, contributes to the action of the leg, since it drives the haunches to the left.

Only when the shifting of the quarters from either leg has become satisfactory can we begin to use the diagonal (the classical) aids for the half-turn on the forehand.

Chapter 6

THE QUESTION OF BALANCE

One of the principal goals of training is the ability to change the horse's equilibrium as circumstances or movements dictate. Since even a competent trainer can only improve natural balance to a certain point, knowing how to recognize it in a horse which you contemplate purchasing is clearly important.

Balance depends on conformation and most particularly on the slope of the shoulder, the orientation of the neck, the formation of the legs and the proportions which make up the harmonious whole. For want of a better definition, we speak of the horse's 'centre of gravity'; but in reality there is no such fixed point in equitation. An animate body keeps this 'centre' in constant motion if only by breathing. There can be no exact method of determining where it is, nor is it possible to fix it in one place. The rider's attention should, therefore, be focused on the consequence of these shifts in the centre of gravity; the balance, in fact, which we shall learn to feel as we become more proficient.

The horse's weight like that of a structure supported on pillars, is distributed over his four legs but, and this complicates matters, it is not evenly distributed because the pillars are not at the four corners, since the neck and head are in front of the forelegs. The weight of these two items and their shape and orientation must therefore influence the over-all weight distribution. Experiments have shown that with a horse weighing 768 lb, holding his head and neck normally, the forelegs carry 420 lb and the hind legs 348 lb; that is, the forelegs carry 72 lb more than the hind legs. The same horse with head and neck lowered, increases the weight carried on his forelegs to 436 lb, his hind legs carrying, as a result, only 332 lb and the difference increasing from 72 to 104 lb.

When head and neck are raised, the weight on the front diminishes to 400 lb whilst that on the back increases to 368 lb, reducing the difference to 32 lb.

Obviously this is something we should think about. When a rider weighing 128 lb sits on his horse in normal fashion 82 lb of his total weight is on the forelegs and 46 lb is carried on the hindlegs. When he leans back, 20 lb is removed from the forelegs to the hind ones.

These figures not only show that neither the horse's own total weight nor the combined weight of horse and rider are evenly divided between fore and hind legs, but that the pro-portion is subject to change by a change of position of the horse's neck and head on one hand and that of the rider's body on the other.

These experiments were carried out with a standing horse on a two-scale balance. But the same weight transfers are ob-tained by variations in the degree to which the hind legs advance under the body. The weight division in two horses of exactly the same weight, for instance, standing with heads and necks in identical positions, is not divided up in the same way, if one is standing stretched out behind and the other is stand-ing with his hind legs well under his body. Thus, if we take a horse with a normal leg formation (i.e. where a plumb line dropped from the point of the buttock meets the point of the hock, follows the cannon and then falls slightly behind the heel) and train him well enough to let us increase the engagement of the hind legs at will, we acquire a means to put more weight on the quarters and thereby lighten the forehand. We can also change the balance by combining this increased engagement of the hind legs with a raising of head and neck, so reducing the distance between these parts and the chest.

This combination is best, because with the horse halted straight the four legs, planted on the ground, form a rectangle called 'the base of sustention' and the smaller this base the more sensitive is the existing balance to change, that is, it becomes easy for horse and rider to play with it, as it were, and the more quickly and smoothly will they be able to pass from movement to movement.

However, and this is fundamental, the pursuit of a better, more sensitive balance must begin with the engagement of the hind legs. Raising the head and neck for *ramener** before this point has the most undesirable repercussions on unprepared quarters. Unfortunately, it is seen all too often because many riders rush to put the front end in what they consider a flattering position, without thinking about the quarters, and the result is usually to the detriment of this propulsive force.

And now a final reminder. Balance must be sought in conjunction with forward movement, the essence of equitation. Neither can be permitted to impair the other.

---

* *Ramener* is an attitude of the head produced by a flexion of the poll, allowed by the joints connecting the first cervical vertebra with the poll and second vertebra, and in which the poll remains the highest point in the overall carriage of the head and neck. In a complete *ramener* the face is held vertical and must not retreat behind this line so that the horse becomes 'overbent'. *Ramener* is produced by the advance of the body towards the head, not by a retraction of the head towards the body. The *ramener* is discussed in detail in the following chapter.

Chapter 7

THE RAMENER

The term *head carriage* is loosely applied to both a natural
and an acquired attitude, but it is incomplete because it does
not include the very important participation of the neck.
Therefore dressage experts keep using the French term
ramener, which has been a part of equestrian terminology for
as long as the concept itself has existed in equitation.

This *ramener* consists of a head position close to the vertical with the poll at the apex and is achieved by driving the
body, and the neck, forward, the hands exerting a measure of
opposition to this forward movement. This leads to a tightening of the angle formed by the first two cervical vertebrae
and poll joints. The hand opposition must be so minimal and
skilful, however, that it 'filters' rather than blocks and, far
from coercing the horse, causes him to yield willingly.

The *ramener,* let me repeat, must be obtained, not by a
retreat of the head towards the body, but BY THE ADVANCE
OF THE BODY TOWARDS THE HEAD, the neck coiled in
strict proportion to the extent to which the head is bent to the
rear.

The pitfall for so many is that this near-vertical position of
the head can, indeed, be obtained both ways, but the results
are not at all alike. And yet it is the result that counts, because
the *ramener* is not an end in itself but a means toward two

ends. These are that it allows the bit to act with the greatest effectiveness on the lower jaw and it 'tautens' the top line of the horse.

In obtaining *ramener* by a retreat of the head we should only be teaching the horse 'to flee the bit', to pass behind it, whereas all training is directed towards teaching him to make contact with it. We want the horse to remain on the bit, even at the halt, yet not allow himself to be carried by it nor to pull against it. By forcing a retreat of the head we would prevent the essential engagement of the hind legs and in doing so prevent the 'engine' from functioning properly. (This brings up the question of using side reins. Properly applied at a trot they may be useful in the hands of an experienced trainer who is able to see whether it is actually the hind legs that are driving the whole horse onto the bit. For the less experienced, however, this is something that is more easily felt from the saddle than seen from the ground.)

In seeking the *ramener* by an advance of the body toward the head, there are two dangers to avoid and a challenge to meet. If we try for *ramener* without the neck being at proper height the horse will overbend; and if we attempt to raise the neck without proper engagement of the hind legs, the base of the neck will cave in, resulting in the opposite of what we require. These are the dangers, the challenge lies in using your own good sense in the day-to-day work. No book can give you guidance on that score. No two horses are built the same way and you must recognize the limitations which may be imposed on your horse by his particular conformation.

The benefits of good *ramener*, obtained by classical means, extend over the entire horse and the finer, more sensitive balance to which it leads gives greater lightness, handiness, and more easily regulated flowing gaits. The accompanying engagement of the hind legs not only shortens the horse 'at the bottom' but, also, from tail to poll, 'at the top'.

I mentioned, as one of the dangers attendant upon obtaining *ramener*, the caving in of the neck. Do not forget that whereas the hind legs are solidly attached to the spine the forelegs have no bony link with it, since the horse lacks a collar bone and the shoulders are held in place by nothing but muscles. If we try to raise the head excessively, the first cervical vertebra, close to the head, is pressed down and in turn presses down on the next one and so on down the line. This will result in a hollowing of the back and the hind legs, incapable of being engaged under the body, being dragged out behind. If, on the contrary, the lowering of the haunches comes about through a correct engagement the hind legs will push not only forward but upward. If this is combined with a *ramener* corresponding to the right neck elevation, the cervical, and consequently all the dorsal and lumbar vertebrae, are stretched. (See Fig. 2).

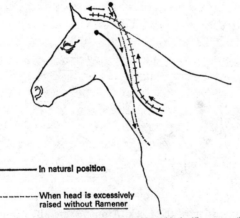

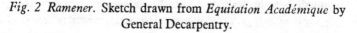

——————— In natural position

------------ When head is excessively
raised <u>without Ramener</u>

++++++++++++ When raised in due proposition <u>with</u> the 'Engagement'
of the hind legs and <u>with</u> the <u>Ramener</u> of the head.

Fig. 2 Ramener. Sketch drawn from *Equitation Académique* by
General Decarpentry.

With almost all young horses, though, and quite a few others, the neck and back muscles must be exercised before we can proceed to the *ramener*. The basic exercise for this is *neck stretching*, effecting not only the neck itself but the back and the hind legs, in fact, the entire animal, whose balance and gaits will be improved in consequence. The principle is simple: at the request of the rider the horse is asked to stretch his neck and head FORWARD AND DOWNWARD. Yet it is a stretch with a difference!

Figures 3 (a) and 3 (b) show you not only the good and the extension, but also why they are good or bad. The way the horses stretches his neck by himself (Fig. 3 (a)) is bad, because

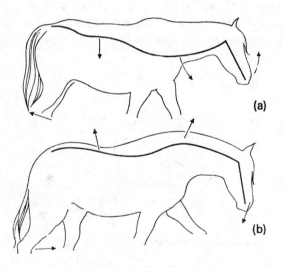

Fig. 3 Extension of the Neck. After a sketch by Major J. Licast. (a) *Natural Extension:* Hind legs *not engaged,* top line not rounded. Base of neck caved in. (b) *Extension requested:* Hind legs *not engaged,* top line rounded. Base of neck raised.

the hind legs do not drive, but just come bumbling after, making the base of the neck cave in. Any *ramener* using this position as a base can only be wrong. Yet if our leg action activates the hind legs they push the whole horse forward, engaging themselves under the mass all the more easily since the stretched and low position of neck and head gives the top line a convex shape (as in Fig. 3 (b)). The exercise is, therefore, dependent on taut reins, which keep the contact throughout the stretching, and on active legs which compel the quarters to become engaged.

But how do we obtain this neck stretching? Simply, by *combing the reins*, i.e. the hands being laid on the reins and sliding backwards alternately. Some of my pupils have found it comes more easily to the watching eyes than to the acting hands, so let me explain how it is done. We take both reins (always on the snaffle bit) near the base of the neck in the right hand, palm down, index finger separating them, the other fingers sufficiently closed to keep them tight. The exact tension and height are optional, but the finger closure must be soft enough to allow the hands to slide easily along the reins (which means that rubber or plaited reins are not practical). As the right hand gets to the end of its run, near our chest, the left takes over, taking hold of the reins at the same place and moving upwards in the same way. When this hand reaches the chest the other takes over and so on. As soon as the horse gives us the merest hint of stretching his neck our hand must yield sufficiently to allow it, without ever losing the permanent contact with the mouth. But all this can be effective only if our legs ACT TO ENGAGE THE HIND LEGS.

This work, started at the walk, is continued at the rising trot at which gait it is most beneficial. Only after the neck muscles are developed and properly oriented may we quite safely tackle the *ramener*.

I have discussed *ramener* and how it is best obtained before describing the work involved in the half-turn on the haunches for a good reason. It is because this movement would lose most of its effect if the neck were extended and stretched more or less downward. Before it can be performed correctly *ramener* must have been obtained.

Chapter 8

THE HALF-TURN ON THE HAUNCHES AND THE HALT

We have seen how the half-turn on the forehand teaches the horse to yield to the action of 'the single leg' and we know that, as is the case with all other aids, the single leg can act, resist or yield. In the half-turn on the forehand it acted to mobilize the haunches now, in the half-turn or the haunches, it resists to keep them in place, a more delicate procedure.

In acting to shift the haunches, a somewhat stronger application of the leg would have caused no great harm; but when the leg resists to maintain the haunches, a force greater than the effort of the horse in trying to shift them in one direction will only result in their being moved in the opposite.

We begin the half-turn on the haunches after that on the forehand because:

(a) By teaching the forehand turn, involving a shift of the quarters from the action of the single leg, we have prepared the horse for the leg which resists an uncalled-for movement of the quarters. It follows that if he has learnt to move away from the lightest pressure of a leg asking for a shift he will respond in like fashion to a resisting leg applied with the same intensity. It is only when we can shift his quarters at will that we are able, also, to resist any unwanted movement made by them.

(b) Most resistances on the part of the horse spring from the haunches, and, for a start, nothing dissolves them better than mobility.

(c) In the half-turn on the forehand at a walk the single leg has compelled the horse to engage the crossing hind, which now gives us the possibility of working either hind at will and so making their engagement as equal as can be. It is easier for the horse to have his hind legs suppled separately, which is something that we cannot do in the half-turn on the haunches.

The half-turn on the haunches does for the shoulders what the turn on the forehand did for the haunches; it gives them lateral mobility. It also re-balances the horse, whose equilibrium was necessarily affected during the half-turn on the forehand, since in any rotation of one end around the other the pivot end is burdened and the turning end lightened to the same extent. If this sounds too technical, think of yourself standing evenly on both feet and getting ready to turn left. To start with you must shift the weight from your right foot onto the left, which is going to be used as a pivot.

By practising both these turning exercises with the horse it follows, providing they are done properly, that the overall balance will be improved. Let us consider, as an example, the half-turn on the haunches from right to left. The procedure for a turn to the opposite direction only involves your reversing the words 'right' and 'left'.

We execute first, an ordinary half-volte on the track to the left, and then, at the very same spot, another smaller one, but still starting off from the track to the left. During the half-circle, the right leg slides back and obliges the haunches to remain on a track inside that made by the forelegs. A right counter-rein requests the shoulders to shift left. Under this action the horse will cross his forelegs, off passing in front of near, a crossing which at first will naturally be no more than minimal.

We make the half-voltes ever smaller, just as we used to do for the half-turn on the forehand, slowing the walk down before the counter-rein asks the shoulders for a lateral shift. This slow-down will be helped if we lean back a bit, and this will also cause us to put more weight on the quarters, which will make it more difficult for the quarters to shift sideways. On the other hand by putting more weight to the rear we shall have lightened the forehand correspondingly, allowing it to move sideways with greater freedom.

If we persist with the exercise, using the same aids, we shall eventually arrive at the half-turn on the haunches on the spot; and here, once more, the four limbs must throughout the movement maintain a regular walk, that is, the pivot leg (the NEAR hind in this case) must execute the time proper to it, on the spot.

It is very important to perfect the half-turns at the walk before attempting them on the spot. The dangers in this movement are far greater than in the half-turn on the forehand where, unless we commit some outrageous error with our hand, there is little chance of the horse backing, since his quarters are in motion. In the turn on the forehand the most common fault is for the haunches to move out sideways because the hind leg, instead of passing over in front of its partner, only moves up to it without crossing. That is bad enough, but it is not nearly as bad as backward motion in the half-turn on the haunches.

If the reins are not taut enough in this movement the horse advances, which is wrong, but if they are too tight he retreats, which is worse. Therefore, the horse must have been carefully prepared for this exercise and the rider himself must have developed sufficient feeling to sense the point to which his hands can oppose the forward movement without causing the horse to back.

The classical aids for the half-turn on the haunches from right to left are as follows. We resist in the shoulders (by stretching the upper body) and draw them back very slightly in order to take some weight off the forehand and put it on the quarters, so preventing the hind legs from slipping out sideways. We use the right counter rein (active aid) to drive the shoulders left; the right single leg (passive aid) keeps the haunches in place; the left leg at the girth maintains impulsion and so keeps the horse on the bit.

In concluding, let me stress the importance, common to both half-turns, of good timing, as it concerns the leg in the former instance and the hand (counter-rein) in the latter.

In either case we ask our horse to cross one leg, fore or hind, in front of the other, whilst all four beats of the walk remain clearly defined. Now, obviously, if we ask for a shift of the crossing leg just when the horse has it on the ground and is leaning on it he cannot move it. Further, if the determining leg or hand action ceases or diminishes considerably at the most propitious moment for the crossing, the horse will either fail to cross his legs altogether or will not be able to cross them sufficiently. If the active aids (single leg in one case, counter-rein in the other) are applied continuously and with unchanging intensity we will get the horse *falling* into the movement, the true gait will be lost and, to add insult to injury, the horse will finally snatch the movement from us, anticipating our request and leaving us impotent to stop it. So it is most important to vary our exercises as soon as the horse has learned to yield to the half-turn aids and so keep them from becoming routine. If we ask, for example, for a complete half-turn, step by step, then for just a couple of steps, followed perhaps by a walk on a straight line before we ask for another one or two steps the horse will never know how many steps he will be required to take at any one time and he cannot indulge in anticipation.

The improvement of even the simplest movement is long-term work, in which some progress may be expected daily but very little on any given day. Beware, above all, of using forcible aids, because the horse unfailingly responds to them by a much superior force of his own. Your physical strength is infinitely less than his, and at this kind of game the rider is always the loser. There is no way in which we can prevail over the horse except by mental education; and the better educated your horse is in this respect the more easily will he be able to cope with the difficulties that arise, within, of course, the limits of his physical capacity.

The Halt In a dressage test the horse must halt straight, remain immobile and keep the contact on the bit. It sounds so very obvious that riders often do not realize just how difficult it is, and so we rarely see a good halt in a test. Yet judges pay particular attention to it because, in part, it is one of the movements which best reveals the quality of training.

Though this movement, as with all others, is not judged by identical standards in tests of different levels and its execution need not, in some of them, be perfect, it must be sufficiently correct to prove that classical principles have been followed in the horse's training.

Some of us are forever tackling feats for which neither we nor our horses are ready and which, in truth, are frequently not expected of us at the level we have reached. I am referring in particular to that over-lightness of the mouth combined with a *ramener* which is way beyond our horses' training level. The result is a horse who, as soon as he is stopped, drops his bit, a serious fault by itself, and then makes matters worse by moving his head. He is then no longer 'on the hand' and is, therefore, at least partially out of control. He is able to shift his legs and, worse of all, to evade contact and overbend.

Like all other movements, the halt is not judged in isolation but by the transitions connecting it with the preceding and following movements. If the horse has dropped his bit the restart into forward movement can only be bad.

The two regions requiring our greatest attention here are the BACK and haunches plus the hind legs. The role of neck and head is secondary on our level, because they are quite passive. All we ask of them is not to do wrong, either by fighting the hand or by going up, a common fault with ewe-necked horses; and if I put most particular emphasis on the back, it is because one tends to forget about it. It is very rightly said that the horse does not travel solely with his four legs, but also with his back. If the back is weak, or poorly suppled, the forces issuing from the 'engine' in the quarters are so badly transmitted to the forehand that its performance must be affected adversely.

If you are lucky enough to own a horse who halts correctly do not imagine for one moment that this has come about by itself; some blessed equestrian Kilroy has been there before you. And if you have a horse of the opposite inclination do not imagine that by repeating poor halts endlessly with this unprepared horse you will one day obtain good ones. He will never be able to give you a decent halt until his back and quarters have been suppled and developed for the movement.

Now let us see how this should be done. By work on the circle, plus serpentines and figure-eights, we first develop LATERAL suppleness and we straighten the horse by working longer and more often on the less satisfactory side. In these exercises the hind legs learn to engage themselves separately and once again we work more frequently on the less efficient leg by placing it on the inside of our circles, etc.

Once this work has borne fruit we proceed to develop LONGITUDINAL suppleness, where both hind legs must engage themselves simultaneously, and initially we do this by speed-ups and slow-downs of the gaits and by passing from walk to trot and back again, eventually including the canter pace.

By opening and closing the key joints of the quarters (sacro-iliac and coxo-femural) they are trained for the requirements of the halt where, after all, the chief and hardest task falls upon them. In speeding up and slowing down, and passing from one gait to another, the horse also learns to move forward freely at the prompting of the leg and to slow down at that of the hand.

If in the course of this work he has come to trust the hand he will not try to evade it in the arena, but will continue to keep a permanent contact on the bit. This is our first goal. Lightness of the mouth comes later, after he has understood that he must remain on the bit.

How do we request the halt? First, we ask for a slow-down of the current gait, commensurate with the horse's degree of training. In the highly schooled horse the slow-down will be virtually imperceptible, but we cannot expect this of a horse below that level. The purpose of this slow-down is twofold: it warns the horse of things to come and prepares him, physically, by a slight re-balancing toward the haunches which engages the hind legs. Our leg and hand aids at this moment must be smooth and gentle but at the same time clear and precise. Once the slow-down has been obtained we close the fingers of both hands, with our shoulders resisting, to obtain the halt, when we loosen our fingers slightly – in other words we yield because the horse has yielded.

During the halt the reins remain sufficiently taut for contact and the legs, also, remain in touch with the horse's sides.

Halting is usually followed by a period of 'immobility', lasting from four to six seconds. The first rule here is for ourselves to remain immobile – often it is the little movement on our part that causes the horse to stir. Do not move anything, neither hands, nor fingers, neither legs nor seat, not even your eyes. I don't mean to say that the act of blinking your eyes will, by itself, make the horse shift but if you fix them on some point you are less likely to make involuntary movements.

Chapter 9

THE REIN BACK AND
REIN AIDS

In equitation we act alike for slowing down and reining back. The legs cease to request the forward movement but stay in contact, then they yield before the hands act alternately by a simple closing of the fingers over the reins. Never forget, however, that this closing of the fingers must be accompanied by a resistance in the shoulders, with your elbows held close to the body. You must not, by advancing the elbows or the upper body, let your arms give what your hands are taking.

The fingerplay resembles the gentle squeezing of juice from two lemons, only it is much, much more gentle. Each hand, in its turn, closes without abruptness as the other opens, and they do so without sawing at the mouth. If you do this properly your horse's head will remain steady and not move from side to side, only the snaffle itself will glide softly over the mouth, making itself felt a little more first on one corner, then on the other. To this alternation of a mere increase and decrease of finger PRESSURES the horse yields easily, whilst to simultaneous TRACTION on both reins he will respond by an opposite and stronger traction of his own. Even if mentally he is still unwilling to yield, he finds it hard to resist for two reasons:

1. His fighting stance against the hand takes the form of a stiffened jaw, a 'clenching of teeth'. But the relaxing effect of

this faint to and fro of the snaffle keeps the mouth soft.

2. To pull at the hand he needs a point to lean on, and the stronger and more solid this point the better can he pull at it. But this hold is refused him by our alternate use of the fingers of each hand under which the point of support can only occur momentarily before disappearing again.

If our legs and hands act in the way described at the ordinary trot, for instance, the horse will slow down the pace. If we persist, the trot will dwindle to its minimum speed and be followed by the walk which in turn will slow to a halt. If our hand action continues, then the horse will start into the rein back.

This is the theory, but the practical problem is somewhat more complex, because an easy, smooth rein back requires preparation and certain longitudinal suppling exercises, one of which happens to be the rein back itself. The main obstacles to a really good rein back are a hollow, feeble back, badly-coupled loins and non-engaged hind legs, the second fault usually being associated with the first. In fact non-engaged hind legs will, buttress-like, stem the retreating motions. But let us have a look at the actual technique of the rein back.

With a horse already trained to rein back the hands alternately exert finger pressures while the shoulders resist, the right hand prompting the retreat of the off diagonal, the left that of the near. The two crucial moments are the start into the rearward movement and the re-start into forward motion.

The rein back from the halt after a few seconds' immobility is rarely required at the level we are discussing, but when it is we must be particularly careful about the halt. The horse must be kept engaged as well as on the bit, that is, he must be halted in good balance, which must not be lost during the period of immobility. So it is essential that we keep him well 'framed' between our hands and legs throughout. Even when no immobility is required the halt must be well defined, but to make the rein back easier we reduce this static period to a minimum.

The intervention of the seat acquires considerable importance here. If we burrow into the saddle, leaning back a bit, the small of the back becomes blocked and this sort of action by the seat will hamper the rein back by being in opposition to the action of the hands. The upper body must remain straight and the seat supple if it is to feel the movement and follow it smoothly.

With a horse not yet trained to rein back it is simplest to start on foot, which is easier for us and the horse, who can comply without being bothered by our weight on his back.

We should face the horse's head, taking a snaffle ring in each hand and letting him place his head at his own height. We push him backward by alternate hand actions but if he will not go back we make him lower his head a little and then repeat the request with our hands while lightly stepping on his feet or pasterns. When he has yielded several times we return to mounted work where, to begin with, we lean more strongly on the stirrups during the movement rather than weighing down on his back and loins.

None of this normally causes too much trouble. The difficulties, indeed, are of a more subtle nature, the foremost of them being the problem of teaching the horse TO BACK WITH HIS BODY WHILE ADVANCING WITH HIS MIND. It must be inculcated into the horse from the start that any backward movement is invariably followed by forward motion, a principle to keep in mind in the work in hand as well as in the saddle. Before we may even think of introducing him to the rein back we must be absolutely sure that free forward movement answers unquestioningly and instantly the action of the legs.

A past Chief Ecuyer at Saumur has given his prescription for the teaching of the rein back as 'teaching the horse not to back'. There is, indeed, a method which obtains the rein back by the legs driving the horse forward onto resisting hands – it is effective but risky, for the reason that it teaches the horse to go back in response to the same leg action which prompts him to go forward. Let us, for Heaven's sake, keep the meaning of simultaneous leg action completely unequivocal: *free forward movement* no more, no less. It must be preferable to a method which involves the risk of confusing the horse in a matter where he may be only too eager to misunderstand.

An added drawback to this last way of reining back is that it is not possible to regulate the exact number of steps. The horse, pushed by the legs, must, when he meets the resisting hand, rein back, so to speak, on his own and we can then have little hope of controlling the movement with any precision. And remember it is 'precision' that counts quite a lot with the dressage judge.

The Five Rein Effects
The opening rein (1st effect) has a natural action upon the horse. It consists of drawing his nose in the direction one wants to take. To turn right, make your right wrist pivot a quarter right turn, thereby turning your nails up, and shift it to the right, keeping your elbows close to the body.

The counter-rein (2nd effect) also called, the neck rein, acts upon the base of the neck which it nudges in the proposed direction. To turn right, make your left wrist act from left to right and from back to front. It is the only rein effect permitting you to manage your horse with a single hand. Unlike the opening rein, the horse, able to evade it without trouble. must be trained to obey it.

Both rein effects act on the forehand which takes the new direction, while the hindquarters are content to follow the shoulders in this change. Since the action does not interfere with the forward movement, the horse does not tend to slow down.

By contrast the following three rein effects address the hindquarters. By a rational disposition of his reins, the rider opposes the shoulders to the haunches, whence their appellation of reins of opposition. This opposition impairs the forward movement which the rider's legs must painstakingly keep intact or restore whenever it tends to disappear; and the effectiveness of these reins is commensurate with the degree of activity the rider creates in the hindquarters.

The direct rein of opposition acts upon the haunches and makes the horse turn right by pushing his haunches to the left. In performing this rein effect, the rider tightens the right rein in the direction of his right knee, after slightly relaxing the fingers of his left hand so as to make the horse understand more easily the action of the right. With this effect the reins remain parallel to the horse's axis.

The right counter-rein of opposition in front of the withers (4th effect) acts upon the shoulders and makes the horse turn left by throwing his shoulders to the left and his haunches to the right; the horse thus pivots around an axis passing approximately through the vertical of the stirrup leathers. In performing this rein effect, the rider, increasing finger pressure on the right rein, shifts his right wrist to the left, passing in front of the withers.

The right counter-rein of opposition passing behind the

withers (5th effect or intermediate rein) acts upon the shoulders and the haunches and displaces the whole horse toward the left. This rein effect is intermediate between the direct rein of opposition, which only acts upon the haunches, and the counter-rein of opposition in front of the withers, which only acts upon the shoulders. It thus falls to the rider, in

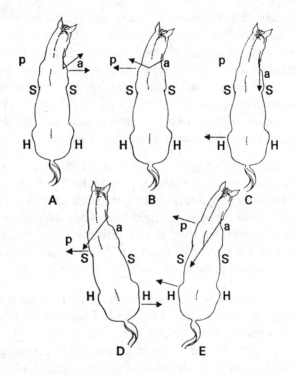

Fig. 4 The Five Rein Effects. (a) The opening rein; (b) The counter-rein; (c) The direct rein of opposition; (d) The right counter-rein of opposition in front of the withers; (e) The right counter-rein of opposition passing behind the withers.

The Co-ordination of the Aids and the Five Rein Effects

	Acting Rein	Forehand	Acting Leg	Hindquarters	New Direction Taken	Aids Applied
I.	Right opening rein	Drawn to the right	Right, pushing the haunches to the left, aiding the right turn.	Pushed to the left	To the right	Lateral*
II.	Right counter-rein	Pushed to the left	Left, pushing the haunches to the right, aiding the left turn.	Pushed to the right	To the left	Diagonal**
III.	Right direct rein of opposition	Turned to the right	Right, reinforcing the action of the right rein which pushes the haunches to the left.	Pushed to the left	To the right	Lateral
IV.	Right counter-rein of opposition in front of the withers; 4th effect	Pushed to the left	Left, reinforcing the action of the right rein which pushes the haunches to the right.	Pushed to the right	To the left	Diagonal
V.	Right counter-rein of opposition behind the withers; 5th effect or intermediate rein	Pushed to the left	Right, reinforcing the action of the right rein which pushes the haunches to the left.	Pushed to the left	The entire horse is Lateral moved to the left.	

* One calls lateral aids the combination of the hand and leg acting on the same side. Example: The right hand and leg are the right lateral aids.
** One calls diagonal aids the combination of the hand of one side and the leg of the opposite. Example: The left hand and right leg.

shifting his right wrist towards the left, to determine how far behind the withers the right rein should pass in order to act with equal intensity upon shoulders and haunches; because the more this intermediate rein tends to approach the direct rein of opposition, the more it acts upon the hindquarters and, on the contrary, the more it tends to approach the counter-rein of opposition in front of the withers, the greater its effect on the forehand.

Chapter 10

CHANGING SPEEDS AND GAITS

This bogeyman of dressage tests should really cause no fear or trouble in the arena if the horse has been worked in the two types of suppling exercises, the lateral and longitudinal ones. Indeed, the latter consist of practically nothing but changes of speed and transitions between gaits.

The lateral suppling exercises are used to straighten the horse as much as possible, whilst the first longitudinal exercises work towards a lowering of the haunches and a consequent engagement of the hind legs. They increase the flexibility of the spine along its length and so develop the play of the sacro-iliac and coxo-femural joints. Although eventually both exercises are practised concurrently we work on lateral suppling first, because the joints affecting the spine usually flex better to the side than lengthways. Additionally, by tackling the more easily accomplished lateral suppleness first we make the longtitudinal work, which follows, easier for our horse. It should be remembered that the horse cannot perform with any real precision in the longitudinal exercises until he is reasonably straight, and that is the purpose of lateral suppling.

LATERAL SUPPLING The principal exercise is the work on the circle, plus serpentines, figures of eight and the negotiating of corners. Though bones, of course, cannot be straightened it is possible, in the young horse, to create in the muscular system a dissymmetry to counteract that of the bones and thus, by compensation, to achieve a measure of straightness.

The principle of the work on the circle or on elements of curves relies on the combined use of both heels and both hands. On a right circle, for example, we use the right leading rein, operating the left rein to limit the bend of the neck and employing, if necessary, a counter-rein effect to push the shoulders to the right. The right leg, around which the horse is bending, is at the girth, whilst the left leg is held slightly back to maintain the haunches and keep them from slipping to the outside, that is, to the left. The theory is quite simple but its application is made more complex because the action of both hands and both legs, each reinforcing all the others, is subject to constant change.

As usual, we shall accomplish more by patient repetition than by hurrying the horse into making tight curves before he is physically capable of performing them. When he bends well on wide circles, and with equal ease to either side, we can then approach the longitudinal suppling period.

LONGITUDINAL SUPPLING. This includes a mixture of speed-ups, slow-downs, changes of gait and finally the rein back, which we have already examined. Now let us see how these variations in the pace at specific gaits are best obtained.

We begin the work at the trot, a gait in which impulsion is greater and more easily preserved than at the walk. The canter, although lending itself to even more impulsion, has two drawbacks. First, the unsymmetrical form of the gait itself causes the horse to be unstraight and secondly its more exciting quality is a hazard to the necessary calm. So we use the trot, the rising trot, which relieves the horse's back, loins and, consequently, his hind legs of the weight they must bear with the rider at the sitting trot. It is necessary to rise to the trot since it is these parts which work hardest in the exercise.

As usual, do not expect too much at first. The hands yield clearly prior to the leg acting, and vice versa. In speeding up, the hands yield, then the legs are applied to produce a speed-up to the degree permitted by the hands. But his 'yielding' of the hands and the time lapse between it and the leg action can vary infinitely. In the early stage, in order to prevent confusion in the horse's mind, the hands must yield completely and only keep a light contact with the mouth, the legs beginning to act only after the hands have yielded entirely. For slowing down the same precautions must be taken, the legs ceasing their action before the hands act.

Once the horse yields perfectly to these simple aids we go on to the next stage involving 'resistance' of the hands in the speed-ups and of the legs in the slow-downs, without thereby losing their clarity as aids. Let us imagine that in speeding up the reins had a tension of *Intensity 10*. We yield to where this intensity dwindles to *3*, but then our hands resist to conserve this *Intensity 3*, while our legs rise progressively from their own initial *Intensity 3* to *Intensity 10*. This is a different story from our early speed-ups, where rein tension was and remained at *Intensity 0*.

For the slow-down it is the same. The legs now yield but stay in contact at *Intensity 3*, while the hands act, progressively bringing rein tension from *Intensity 3* to *Intensity 10*. As our horse is making progress, the time lapse between leg and hand action dwindles, *without ever vanishing completely*.

When these speed-ups and slow-downs are performed well at the trot, they can be practised at walk and canter. Still later in the training we pass from gait to gait: ordinary walk, slow walk, ordinary trot, strong trot, slow trot, extended walk, ordinary trot, ordinary canter, etc., until eventually we can include the rein back in these transitions and at the very end, the halt. It is in passing from rein back to walk, to trot, to canter, and back again, reducing to a minimum the dead time between the retrograde and forward movements, that we attain the height of longitudinal suppling.

Chapter 11

THE CANTER

At this stage in our training programme the work at the canter pursues two aims – easy departures into the gait and a straight horse at the strike-off and during the canter. Here, even more than elsewhere, it is a question of educating the horse's reflexes by psychological rather than physical means.

The means at our disposal are various, and their choice depends on a 'diagnosis', much as one medicine will be efficacious in treating a certain disease whilst another will be necessary for a different ailment. If the physician errs in his diagnosis the remedy can, of course, turn out to be worse than the illness it was supposed to cure. The simile can be taken even further: one particular patient's reaction to an appropriate drug, for instance, may be so unfavourable that a change in the treatment will be required. Similarly, whilst we should use certain classical methods which will apply roughly to all horses, we must not allow ourselves to become inflexible towards the individual in our application of them.

Although the canter is dependent on mental education, it also relies upon balance. A favourable balance for the canter facilitates the mental education and, conversely, a good mental education helps to solve the problems of balance, because it predisposes the horse to seek his right balance at the strike-off.

To begin at the beginning we will take the case of a young horse. In the school we obtain the first canters by riding the rising trot on the INSIDE DIAGONAL (i.e. the rider sitting in the saddle as the left diagonal – left fore and right hind – comes to the ground on the circle left, and vice versa) and causing the horse to accelerate beyond the maximum trotting speed, with the result that he ends up by losing his balance and 'falling' into the canter. We should attempt these first strike-offs into canter in the corner of the school where the turn will precipitate the loss of balance. When the horse has reached the point where he will 'fall' into the canter on the 'inside' lead on both reins we carry out the exercise outdoors using the same procedure, but without employing corners. We do not check to trot or walk too promptly but let him canter on for a few minutes with maximum freedom of neck, but without losing contact with the bit. If he goes too fast we slow him down by the voice, not the reins. This exercise is meant to let him find his cantering balance under our weight, and the various intonations of our voice should have acquired sufficient meaning for him during the first few weeks of lunging at walk and trot to give us the control we need. We must be careful to do just about an equal amount of work on both leads with merely a little extra practice being given on the lead he finds more difficult.

After some time we need no longer stay on straight lines but can request a few easy changes of direction on wide curves. After five or six weeks of this, with the rider remaining as passive as possible, we can return to lunging work, asking for departures at the canter from the trot and walk by using our voice assisted by the lunging whip. Concentrate at this point on giving the command at precisely the right moment until he canters on the word of command alone, without our having to use the whip. Once this can be obtained we mount again. Both legs must now act as evenly as possible and with equal intensity, just sufficient enough to impart the necessary impulsion which the hands will control. The actual strike-off into canter can be asked for by the voice, to which the horse is accustomed, and it is surprising how easily it will be obtained if the balance is fairly correct.

Now we must get such departures by our physical aids alone. For the left canter, the right leg slides slightly back and the left is held at the girth whilst the hands keep the horse's neck as straight as possible. At first the voice accompanies the aids but gradually we can dispense with its help. What is important is the double role of the outside leg: it signals to the horse that a departure on the inside lead is in the offing and at the same time prevents the haunches from being thrown to the outside, that is, into the position they would assume for the canter on the opposite lead. It is the inside leg which, acting at the girth with light pressures, actually prompts the canter.

If the outside leg action is too strong it will cause the horse to become crooked, particularly if his natural bend is to the left. This is the inherent bend of the canter, and when it occurs in this fashion the crookedness is that much more accentuated. Though we have no room in this outline to discuss the reasons for all these inflections there is no wishing them away and they are blatantly apparent to any judge in any test.

If your horse almost invariably strikes off into the left canter when your aids demand the right, use the wall to help you straighten him out. The root of the evil lies in the haunches dropping off to the left, a position conducive to the left canter. Therefore, track to the right and before applying the aids for the canter depart on the off lead, shift both wrists to the left whilst keeping the neck straight. In doing this, you place *the shoulders in front of the haunches.* The horse is then straight, or at least relatively so, and the haunches cannot escape to the left because the wall contains them far more efficaciously than could your left leg. There are several advantages to this procedure: first of all, you accustom your horse to striking off into the right canter straight, not crooked; secondly, your hand action, affecting the forehand, allows you to see the resulting position, whilst leg action, affecting the haunches, cannot be seen and you will not be able to judge the horse's overall position. Last, but not least, the rule in classical equitation is to straighten a horse by re-setting the SHOULDERS IN FRONT OF THE HAUNCHES, not vice versa.

Straightening the horse during the canter is even harder than at trot and walk and requires exercises well beyond our current scope and ability. What we must not do, however, in our first dressage tests is to aggravate the horse's bend by awkward aids. If you are on the left circle, for example, remember that your OUTSIDE leg is to give nothing but a warning signal for the departure at the left canter, that it is, so to speak, a 'position leg', not an 'action leg'. The acting leg, which prompts the departure, is the left one, which by being positioned at the girth cannot possibly cause the haunches to deviate. In this way your departures, even if they are not absolutely straight, will be correct by the standards of low-level dressage tests. Once the departure into canter has been obtained the outside leg remains slightly behind its normal place, but it is not used for impulsion. This remains the business of the inside leg which, because it is at the girth, is in no danger of tampering with the straightness of your horse. And while you are on the circle, remember that you use hand action to align shoulders with haunches, not leg action to align haunches with shoulders.

At the ordinary left canter you must 'cadence' your gait by holding your left hand a little higher than the right, slightly opening and closing its fingers over the rein in rhythm with the movement. Act, indeed, as though your hand had to permit each stride.

If you wish to slow down, resist with your shoulders and lengthen the time your fingers are closed so that your hand tells the horse, 'Not so fast, slow down, wait for permission for the next stride.' Conversely, if you want to push up to the strong canter lower this same hand, letting your fingers go almost limp. If the horse has been well trained, he ought to speed up of his own accord without needing increased leg action.

Establishing such understandings between horse and rider is a good policy; it prevents extreme responses due to insufficient or excessive leg action and, since the horse accelerates on his own, although with his rider's permission, the speed-ups are prompt but unhurried.

Whilst training for this stronger canter, at first use the spurs at the moment when the yielding hand goes down. The horse will then quickly understand that he should accelerate as soon as the hand permits. This is a good example of educated reflexes making for a 'vibrant' and 'forward' horse.

The seat must, of course, follow the canter motion if you wish to maintain complete contact with your horse, but (and it is a big BUT) this movement should be limited to the seat itself and it should stop at the waist. Unless the upper body, primarily the shoulders, remains absolutely still your position becomes awkward and, which is worse, it gives the judges the impression that your horse is so sluggish to the legs that your seat must keep pushing for all it is worth. Don't push in this way, and when you have to check to the trot don't push at all, just follow the movement. If you push the horse lets the canter dwindle to and beyond its minimum speed, thus reaching the trot somewhere beyond the specified point. Alas, the adage 'Better late than never' is not one that is appreciated by judges.

The Counter Canter Used at home for training, the counter-canter (employing the opposite lead, i.e. right lead on circle left, and vice-versa) supples the horse, improves his balance and straightens his true canter to whatever degree this may be possible. In dressage tests it demonstrates the extent of suppleness and balance and the obedience to the aids. In either case, any forcible persuasion, however slight, is wrong. In training because it would make us lose the benefits accruing from the exercise and during a test because it would cost us marks. Coercion in the execution of the counter-canter is particularly obvious because it is one of the movements where, even if we camouflage certain actions of our own, we cannot camouflage the horse's reactions to them. Judges tend to be all the more severe in these cases because in itself the counter-canter is not difficult. Though some call the counter-canter 'unnatural' and purposeless it is not so, being the natural complement of the other work at the canter.

We only need look at horses cantering spontaneously at liberty to see that, aside from a very few who are 'ambidextrous', most will favour a given leg and when there is sufficient space will gaily negotiate turns on their favourite lead, even though it be a false canter, changing only if their balance is jeopardized by the speed of their approach. To be honest, however, it is not this false canter we are looking for. In dressage tests the horse is expected to counter-canter on either lead, not as he does at liberty to canter on the lead he is more comfortable on. So our training aim is to render him equally skilful on both leads.

The progression leading to counter-canter is as follows. Once the general training has reached a point where we can control our horse without forcible aids of any sort we ride him in long canters at the speed most comfortable to him; accustoming him to cantering as easily on one lead as on the other but working longer and more often on the problem lead. When the departures at the canter are as easy to obtain on one lead as on the other, when we feel the back muscles are relaxed under our seat and the movement is quite effortless and supple, then, and only then, can we begin to introduce the counter-canter. It is better to start the exercise outside where walls and turns do not compel us to take one direction when it might be better for the horse's education to take another.

Riding on the left lead, on a barely perceptible curve, we first ask for change of direction to the right, then to the left, and then again to the right. We should not intensify the aids at the moment of change to the right but if we feel him about to become disunited or in danger of changing his leading leg we must turn to the left rather than put him off balance and interrupt the smoothness of the gait. If, as happens at times, we cannot prevent a change of lead or a disunited canter then we must check to the walk and then depart in canter on the same lead at the very spot where the mishap occurred. No punishment can be contemplated at this stage.

We do this every day, tightening, as progress allows, the curves at the counter-canter to the point required in the tests for which we are preparing. The hands are the sole aids in the various changes of direction, the legs doing no more than to preserve and maintain impulsion, being used simultaneously and with an absolutely even pressure. If one leg is stronger than the other we risk interfering with the gait and prompting a change of lead. The right counter-rein effects the left turn on the near lead, the right direct rein of opposition the right turn at the left counter-canter and, of course, vice versa. Be careful to keep the seat still, if it is allowed to shift the horse can easily become confused.

These are the secrets of the counter-canter but in the last analysis it is a question of the rider giving the utmost liberty to the horse whilst he himself, beyond giving minimal directives, remains passive. Ridden in this way the horse will not stiffen up during the performance which would be a sure sign that he was fighting his rider. All that is really required of the latter is an ability to feel whether or not his horse is ready to give what is about to be asked. It is the kind of 'feel for the horse' which is essentially the art of horsemanship.

One particular problem in the counter-canter is perhaps the general canter problem of neck inflection. Ideally, the horse should be straight, but this standard is not required at the level we are discussing. A slight inflection to the side of the lead is allowable, because in giving the horse a certain necessary balance it allows and helps him to hold his canter and prevents his making an ill-timed change. In addition it makes the weight flow back to the opposite shoulder, thus lightening the shoulder on the lead-side, a very welcome occurrence at a moment when we wish to help the lead-side and hold back the other.

Chapter 12

THE SECOND AND THIRD
COMMANDMENTS

Impulsion is an important point under the heading GENERAL
IMPRESSIONS on the score sheet. Consciously or otherwise,
the judges' marks in this respect are a compound of the impulsion, or lack of it, underlying each single movement. Since
none of these can be quite correct without sufficient impulsion you may be sure that if there are a dozen movements in
the test the final mark on the score sheet is the sum total of a
dozen mental notes. But what is impulsion? In the first place,
although people tend to use the two terms interchangeably,
impulsion is not the same as forward movement. Forward
movement is a physical motion, impulsion is a moral quality.
A horse can advance at walk, trot or canter without an ounce
of impulsion being present. Conversely, in the *piaffe*, for instance, which requires impulsion without advance, he trots on
the spot, yet is ready and eager to go forward at the slightest
prompting. The hall-mark of impulsion is to be found in the
really well-trained horse who will even rein back under impulsion.

The most apt of the many metaphors which seek to define
impulsion as distinct from forward movement seems to be
that of the steam boiler, which generates energy (forward
movement) only if the steam (impulsion) can be channelled
through a controlling valve (the hands). All horses have, in

varying degrees, some natural impulsion and it is the development and control of this quality which is a principle aim in
training.

With few exceptions forward movement is obtained by legs
alone, but impulsion requires legs plus hands, the two acting
alternately and never simultaneously. The legs create and/or
increase the impulsion; the hands either store it or allow it to
transform itself into speed.

You will remember that the trainer's FIRST COM-
MANDMENT prescribes CALM. Once the young horse, by ac-
quiring calmness, has come to trust the trainer, the SECOND
COMMANDMENT – FORWARD occupies the trainer's attention. The horse is worked on the lunge line and with the
lunging whip. Gradually as the horse learns to associate the
whip and click of the tongue we proceed, possibly after some
weeks, to mounted work, in order to get the horse to understand the meaning of leg action. Once more, the best and
simplest means to employ with the young horse is to get him
to associate a request to go forward with the whip rather than
the spurs; and this is just as valid for your trained horse.
Whenever you have trouble with the forward movement the
sting of the whip is a more effective incitement than the prick
of the spur.

Holding both reins evenly in a single hand, your legs request the forward movement and are followed up instantly by
a whiplash just behind your leg. Your horse will almost certainly bound forward! Let him do so and pat him immediately. Do not rein in too soon but let him canter a good
hundred yards before gently calming him by voice to a slow-
down. After a few minutes' rest, on long reins, repeat the
exercise, then send him back to the stables. I lay any odds that
at your next ride he will spring forward at the slightest
prompting of your legs.

It is a simple recipe within the means of any rider, but, as is the case with any recipe, the final quality of the dish depends on the quality of the ingredients. So remember the order in which the aids are applied. The leg action must be clearly defined but not too strong; the rein hand must advance sufficiently for it to ensure that the horse meets no resistance when he bounds forward; finally, the whiplash must come down energetically a split second after the leg action, without waiting for any reaction to the leg signal. As soon as the horse moves forward vigorously, pat him, without waiting for a slow-down to the walk. You should, incidentally, be quite sure that your seat is sufficiently strong to keep you in the saddle no matter how violent your student's reaction to this 'lesson of the legs'. If you can't stay with him you teach the horse the quite counter-productive lesson that you can be shaken off, open entirely new horizons to his innocence and tell him what to do with a cumbersome and annoying weight on his back. This lesson of the legs should be given several times whenever the horse seems to be getting unresponsive to their use.

So far so good, but what if the hands keep destroying what the legs have so painstakingly wrought? Not only will the entire work have to be redone but after a few repeated mistakes by the hand your horse will become fed-up with the whole affair. It is then your fault. You have dulled his spirit just as a carefully sharpened knife of fine steel will soon be dulled if used to chop wood. Resharpened it will cut again, but too many sharpenings whittle away the blade. So let your hands be, remain light, content to 'indicate' – no more. In any disagreement with your horse, have recourse to your legs and tone down the effect of your hands. Three-quarters of all resistances are caused by the hands – hands that are too hard. Keeping your horse ever fresh to the legs, ever keen to advance, will avoid all kinds of trouble.

As for the THIRD COMMANDMENT, the degree of STRAIGHTNESS necessary in dressage depends on the standard of the test and nowhere on your score sheet will you find the actual word spelled out. Yet straightness, or the lack of it, has profound repercussions on the *gaits*, on lightness and on the ease shown in the execution of the movements.

To many a straight horse is the one whose haunches, in following a straight line, do not fall to right or left and do not shift. This is nothing less than the truth, but it is not all of it.

Admittedly, the horse is not naturally straight, any more than you and I. In fact, only three out of a thousand human beings have a perfectly straight spine. Lack of straightness in the horse is due to the fact that one side is convex and the other, usually the near side, is concave. This natural bend in the horse is aggravated by our own habits. By approaching, bridling, saddling and leading from the near side we get him into the habit of looking left more often than right. Except for the south-paws among us, we tend to lunge him more often to the left, and, also, if you have been around riding schools, you may have noticed that more often than not all the riders are on the left rein and that they stay on it longer than they do on the right.

Furthermore, horses themselves are seldom ambidextrous. They prefer to canter on the near lead, they perform the half-pass more easily from right to left and do half-turns on the forehand better when the haunches are driven to the left, and so on. If we do not watch out for this from the beginning this additional factor, leading to greater crookedness, gets worse and worse.

To give an example: a rider who is more comfortable on the off diagonal, trots longer on it than on the other up to the point where the horse himself takes to casting him back onto the habitual diagonal, should the rider ever manage to get on the opposite one, by putting in a false beat. Since this gets worse with time, routine and age we should when buying an already trained or partly trained horse be particularly careful to pick one that is straight or almost so.

Actually, a horse is really straight when, following a straight course, the line of his spine (from poll to tail) corresponds with the line of travel, with both lateral pairs of legs being carried equally on either side of this line. The same is true when following a curve, when the bend of not only the neck but of the entire body is even and harmonious and each hind leg touches down on the track of the corresponding fore. Once this is so haunches and shoulders are so placed as to assure the straightness of their relative movement, weight distribution is regular, the forces of quarters and forehand harmonize, resistance vanishes and the horse is light.

The Three Commandments – CALM, FORWARD and STRAIGHT – must be ever foremost in your mind, whatever the movement you are working on. All three are equally important, but the order of enforcement calls for calm first, and this calm, unlike the other two requisites, must be complete in any kind of riding. Then comes the forward movement, without which we could not make use of, and control, the impulsive forces which are destined to become an instrument in straightening the horse.

Chapter 13

WORK ON TWO TRACKS

Two-track work, which comprises several movements, derives its name from the fact that the fore and hind legs follow different tracks, while in one-track work both follow the same. To save misunderstandings let us make it clear that neither term should be taken literally. In reality, one-track work, where the hind follow the fore legs in perfectly straight alignment, produces two tracks, one for each lateral pair of legs. Half-pass and shoulder-in, the principal two-track exercises, really produce four tracks, one for each leg.

In SHOULDER-IN the horse is bent, travelling sideways yet always forward in the direction of his convex side. The legs of the concave (near side in the left shoulder-in) cross in front of those of the convex side. The HALF-PASS, in its classical form, has the horse straight (rectilineal) from head to dock, except for a slight bend of the head in the direction of the movement (left in the left half-pass). This bend of the head should be sufficient just to let the rider see the corner of the eye on the inflected side. For all its slightness, this bend has a repercussion on the entire spine, causing it to take on an even less perceptible bend which adds to the horse's grace and helps to draw along the outside shoulder. It is the outside shoulder, of course, which does most of the work.

In both movements the main pitfall is an easily detectable

loss of impulsion, since the horse noticeably slows down just as he goes from one-track into two-track motion. Remember, here as elsewhere, good impulsion is basic! Another rule to remember is that the crossed leg regulates the work of the crossing one in the half-pass.

What actual purpose has the work on two tracks? Well, most particularly, it supples and strengthens the dorsal and lumbar muscles, by causing them to play in an unusual direction. It also lightens the forehand and engages the hind legs, so improving balance and making the horse more agile, and, as well, it gives him the ability to change this balance effortlessly.

And what kind of progression should we follow? Let me say first of all that we should not even start one before the horse can yield easily to the single leg shifting the haunches. To teach him to cross his hind legs correctly we have already practised half-voltes in reverse, shifting the haunches, and we have reached the point where in half-voltes, holding the haunches with the leg, we can shift the shoulders by a counter-rein so that the forelegs cross while advancing in the same way as the hind legs do in the half-voltes in reverse. As I explained, this led naturally into the half-turns on forehand and haunches. In other words, we should at this stage be able to obtain half-passes, independently so to speak, from both fore and hind legs. The problem we now have is 'to put both ends together'.

Not only have we obtained this lateral mobility of forehand and quarters with the legs crossing, but we have also taught the horse to bend in exercises on the circle, which is so important in obtaining a true half-pass. In the half-pass to the left, for example, the head is bent to the left and the horse moves left and FORWARD, the off fore and off hind crossing in front of the near legs. But we must appreciate that the further the near hind advances under the body the greater is the strain imposed on the off hind in making the cross-over. If the horse avoids making this effort he will hold back with his near hind and move it sideways. This will cause a considerable loss of forward movement, since the release of the near hind no longer drives him sufficiently ahead and in this instance the improvement in engagement expected from the work on two tracks will not be realized. But the work on the circle has taught the horse to engage his inside hind which thus supports the mass and we are now able to control this engagement with our inside leg at the girth. Just as half-voltes and half-voltes in reverse were at the root of the crossing work, so the work on the circle is at the root of the engagement of the inside hind.

So we can begin the two-track work properly by using the shoulder-in, the horse's ultimate preparation for the half-pass. We work in this order because the bend of the horse's whole body and the direction he follows in the shoulder-in puts a greater crossing strain on the forelegs which in any case experience more difficulty in crossing than the hind. Additionally, the aids for shoulder-in are easier from the rider's viewpoint than those for the half-pass.

The Two-track Movements

SHOULDER-IN In the shoulder-in the horse must be UNI-FORMLY bent from head to dock to one side while moving forward in the opposite direction. This inward curve must initially be extremely slight, but it must be even throughout the horse's length and the tracks made by the fore and hind legs must be quite distinct. Too often we see excessively curved necks with almost straight bodies, with the result that we get a 'broken' base to the neck which frustrates any effect of the 'active' rein on the quarters.

The application of the aids for, let us say, the left shoulder-in is as follows: The left counter-rein of opposition passing behind the withers shifts shoulders and haunches to the right equally, if, of course, the hand is properly placed; the horse is then bent to the left. In order to limit the inflection given to the neck by this left rein, *the right hand*, after yielding, resists to maintain the required degree of inflection. *The right leg*, slightly behind its normal place, keeps the rightward shift of the haunches from becoming exaggerated, then it yields as needed when the haunches remain in position and in the correct relation to the overall inflection. The leg resists to oppose any excessive movement to the right which threatens to change the inflection. The primary purpose of the left leg is to maintain impulsion whilst, incidentally, reinforcing the action of the left rein by driving the haunches to the right.

In dressage tests the rider begins and ends the shoulder-in at a given spot, starting from either a straight or a curved line. In training, however, it is preferable to start from the circle for two important reasons. First, it lets us bend the horse in accordance with the chosen curve – the wider the circle, the less the bend – and secondly, it gives us plenty of time to prepare him. Actually, if the horse is still not ready after one circle there is nothing to prevent us from riding a second one at the same place. Besides this, when we return to ordinary one-track motion on the straight line after a few steps of shoulder-in (three or four at most in the early phase) the bend is lost and the horse has to be prepared all over again for the next few steps. When we want to stop the shoulder-in we keep the bend, using a circle as the base, and simply drive the horse forward on the circle which we have already begun.

Here is what happens when we put the horse into the left shoulder-in. On the track to the left, we describe a wide left-handed circle to obtain a slight overall bend from poll to tail and we keep riding the circle until the horse has achieved the bend we want and is correctly positioned for the movement. Once he is moving in this proper bend we request the shoulder-in by applying the left counter-rein of opposition passing behind the withers at the precise moment when the forelegs are leaving the track, and whilst the hind legs are still on it. We execute three, four, five steps of shoulder-in, then put the horse forward again by ceasing the left rein action and pushing him ahead on the circle which we have already started. We can then repeat the exercise as we wish.

I hope I have now made it clear that during the entire period, whether we are on one or two tracks, the horse remains in the same bend, so that the exercise may be continued or discontinued quite easily at any moment. Setting off from a straight line instead of from a circle makes it necessary for us to put the horse in the correct bend in a split second. This is always difficult to accomplish successfully and with a young horse it is really impossible. Then, of course, when operating from the straight line we must inevitably, as we return to it, lose the bend and be forced to request it again the next time we want our few steps at shoulder-in.

This bend, the proper poll to tail bend, is the essence of the shoulder-in and it is more important in the early stages than even the extent to which the legs cross. With practice the correct and full crossing of the legs can be easily enough developed.

HALF-PASS By exercising the horse in oblique travel in the shoulder-in we make him agile and obedient to reins and heels. Having reached this point we can then introduce the half-pass. Once more, the extent to which the horse is inclined obliquely must at first be minimal and must never exceed 30–40 degrees or, at the very outside, 45 degrees.

86

One can begin by the head to the wall exercise but, whilst this helps us judge the exact degree of obliquity and lets us use the wall to hold the horse's legs on the respective tracks, it has the drawback of encouraging the horse to slow down when starting into the half-pass. It is much better to begin by riding the half-volte, holding the haunches with the legs and returning to the track by two or three steps of the half-pass. Far from detracting from the forward movement the return to the track, in fact, is a means of promoting it. The half-volte also, and most usefully, prevents us from making any excessive demand.

The aids for the half-pass to the left are as follows. *Right counter-rein*, to drive the shoulders to the left, *right leg*, held slightly back, to drive the haunches to the left, *left rein* giving the head inflection to the left and regulating the gait in co-ordination with the right. The *left leg* maintains impulsion and watches over the engagement of the near-hind and the *body weight* is placed more upon the left buttock and stirrup.

After this exercise on the half-volte we can, indeed, go on to head to the wall, and when this is done correctly and easily we can make a further improvement by employing tail to the wall, so that the wall no longer guides us or our horse and our aids alone keep the legs on their respective tracks.

Still later comes the half-pass on the diagonal, in which the dangers of anticipation can so easily arise. The haunches can either laterally anticipate the shoulders and/or the horse himself can anticipate the movement and even take charge of it. The last may be avoided by never half-passing the full length of the diagonal and never requesting the same number of steps twice in succession. We might begin the half-pass, for instance, coming out of the corner, execute three or four steps, walk straight for a varying number of steps, continue the half-pass in the same direction for two more steps and

G 87

then once more walk straight. In this way the horse is obliged to be ever alert to the aids and he never dares anticipate.

The last phase of half-pass work consists of counter-changes of hand, which are nothing but a combination of a half-pass in one direction followed, without a transitional break, by another to the opposite side. Since the previous work, progressively reducing the direct travel between half-passes, has rendered the horse obedient and light to legs and hand he should be capable of swift changes of balance on his own. All we need do to accomplish counter-changes of hand is to straighten our horse completely during the last half-pass step and start into the first step of the half-pass in the opposite direction by first driving the shoulders in the new direction. We would do well for now to refrain from intervening with the leg in charge of driving the haunches, lest it cause them to precede the shoulders, which is a very serious fault!

Chapter 14

GENERAL IMPRESSIONS

Most of you will have had some show experience prior to entering dressage or combined training tests. In show-jumping competitions you expect the horse to make a somewhat greater effort on the day of competition than during training sessions. After all, it is only a matter of a little more of the same stuff, the fences being a little higher here and a little wider there. In fact, each successive show is really part of the training progression.

But this is not the case in the dressage test, which probes not so much *what* your horse has learned to do but *how* he has learned to do it and with how much ease, suppleness, lightness and freedom. These four points are indeed among those on the score sheet under GENERAL IMPRESSIONS and you will always get better marks if you take the horse to the standard of test where, rather than having to ask him for a little more than in everyday work, you can ask him for a little less than he is really capable of producing.

In show-jumping there were two ways of making time: first by not losing any, then by gaining some. In dressage tests, too, there are important omissions and commissions, errors easy to avoid and finishing touches to work out prior to presentation. Some of them are small points but, nevertheless, they can make the difference between success and failure.

Dressage riders would learn a lot if they had a chance to watch a test from the judge's seat. They would then see the movements from a different angle and better understand the importance of certain details. From his vantage point the judge can see the whole arena: four sides, four straight angles, the letters dividing it and the centre line running in front of his seat. Everything is straight and perfectly visible on this carefully prepared piece of ground on which you, the competitor, have to ride. You make your entrance on the centre line, coming to a halt at X, saluting the judge and departing to begin your test from this exact and conspicuous point in the empty rectangle. Have you ever thought that the judge's attitude for the next few minutes will be conditioned, favourably or otherwise, by this arrival, halt and departure from X?

Too many of you act as though these three simple (but not easy) movements were not an integral part of the test. There is a certain *laisser-aller* about this part of the test; the horse does not arrive straight, he halts on the instalment plan and not with any noticeable straightness either and he ambles off again as though it really didn't matter. The judge may not mark this first movement too severely, it is true, unless it actually approaches the above extreme, but you have alerted him to what might follow and at the very first fault the blow will fall.

As you enter at the trot or canter you must give the judge the impression that you have the situation and your horse both well in hand. 'Give the impression' does not mean 'bluff'; the self-assurance must be real, but it must, also, be apparent. Aside from the psychological effect on the judge, the movements will be more correct, the horse will obey your aids better and your adherence to the requirements of the test will be far superior. In sum, while you should not be a show-off, your bearing on horseback should be a show-off's dream.

Other items listed under GENERAL IMPRESSIONS on the score sheet are *position* and *aids*.

The position, which we have already discussed, must be classical. It must give the appearance of being utterly habitual and infinitely comfortable. Indeed not only must it look so but it must *be* so if you want to do your test precisely and smoothly.

Watch your head: look high and far ahead when on a straight line; in changing direction look at the point where you want to go before letting your hands and legs act, and on a circle do not forget to advance your outside shoulder a bit to keep facing the direction in which you are going, so that you are not left behind the horse's movement.

Your use of aids should be correct, that is, efficacious, accurate and discreet. If they fulfil all three requirements the judge will recognize them as the fruit of long and patient homework and good training of both rider and horse, that has resulted in an obvious mutual trust. Any improvisation during the test, however brilliant, only serves to produce confusion and disorder.

Watch your legs: they usually move too much. 'Rocked' by the cadence of the trot they can give the impression that you *must* push your mount incessantly. If, in fact, you really have to push him, do so by lively but brief actions, making sure they are not so lively that he jumps out of his skin.

Let me give you an additional tip which you can make use of when you are in certain parts of the arena. Since the judge sits behind letter C, if you are on the right rein, say, between B–A–C, it follows that it is impossible for him to see your left leg, but he has a jolly good view of the right one. Therefore, keep the right leg still and use the left! It takes reasonable tact, of course, to prevent the horse from giving you away, since if your action is too strong he is prone to let the cat out of the bag.

If your aids are to be discreet without loss of efficacy you must learn to 'prepare' your horse in good time. The more accurately you are able to choose the right moment and the right manner for this preparation the better the movement to follow will be, the more easily will it be obtained and the more natural will be the ultimate execution. Except in the case of an insufficiently trained or a highly-strung horse, loss of calm is caused by the horse being 'surprised' by the aids.

If you shout the command 'Quick March' at a squad of soldiers standing 'at ease' the result will be chaotic. If you prepare them for the order by first bringing them to attention and then giving them a preliminary warning of the command which is to follow they will move off smoothly and precisely. It is exactly the same with the horse.

The Art of Passing and Accepting Judgement Schooling a horse for dressage tests requires daily work over a prolonged period and is probably less enjoyable than sailing over fences when training a jumper. Aspiring dressage riders, commendably and necessarily, do not mind this painstaking preparation, but their one horror seems to be the actual riding of the test. I think, perhaps, it is the dread of the unknown, of the intangible. Unlike show-jumping or cross-country, where the faults incurred are entirely incontestible, the dressage arena cannot reveal faults in this way. Marks depend on the quality, or lack of it, in executing a series of movements and this is something which cannot approach the 'black and white' of the dislodged pole or the deliberate refusal. It is sometimes very difficult for a rider to understand the mark for a particular movement, but if you tend to feel sorry for yourself and hard done by let me assure you that it is not all plain sailing for the judge either. Even in the great international competitions, where he can comfortably score on the basis of a firm standard of 'perfection', defined for him by the rules of the Fédération Equestre Internationale, we find differences, usually negligible but sometimes not, in the scoring of three judges. Though this situation is definitely open to improvement, absolute agreement is probably impossible on this earth, since two, let alone three, people will never feel exactly the same way about anything. There is also the long period of time over which total concentration is required of the judges if they are to observe every movement made by horse and rider with equal thoroughness. Naturally the capacity for prolonged concentration will vary from one judge to another, although all should possess it to an acceptable degree.

In the official F.E.I. test for the Three-Day Event, where certain movements must be performed at the collected trot, there is no indication which would help the judges to determine the degree of collection required, though it is obvious that it is not meant to be the equal of that required in the Grand Prix de Dressage. In tests at a lower level things become even more complicated for the judge. He no longer has 'absolute' perfection for his yardstick in anything, but is left with nothing more precise than a 'relative' perfection, theoretically dictated by the test level itself but in practice largely left to his own interpretation. His actual base, in fact, is pathetically fluid.

Take a test of medium difficulty performed by twenty riders. The judge knows the standard of the test, but not of the riders and horses. Some of them are sure to be very good, some will be pretty bad, and the majority will be of medium standard. This state of affairs is bound to be reflected in his scoring, and usually is. Suppose his marks for the first entries are either fairly high or fairly low, how far up or down will this initial judgment push his marks as better or worse riders come onto the scene?

I know that this predicament could be avoided by using the same judge, who knows most of the horses and riders, time after time. But then again, we find ourselves between the devil and the deep blue sea, because this judge, scrupulously objective though he may be, is human, not a robot, and he cannot entirely rid his subconscious mind of past impressions.

Anyway, in practice it is nearly impossible to secure such continuity, even if it were desirable. Normally the judge is unfamiliar with contestants and horses and must play it by ear as the first three or four riders perform, waiting to gain a general impression of the true level of the class he is judging. Then, if the general execution of a movement (such as departures at the canter, counter-canter work, halts, rein backs, etc.) happens to be fair to middling, but good in one or two cases, he will tend to score these two performances a little higher than is warranted by their actual quality. Those two fortunates will score a 9 or even 10 but they should not be deluded by this very relative mark into believing that the movement in question is no longer subject to improvement.

Hence, judges' marks must be interpreted bearing in mind their double meaning – the value of the movement within the context of the test and within that of the group performing it. For these reasons we can gain only a very tentative notion of the true value of a performance by comparing two or three score sheets of equivalent tests ridden at different venues and under different judges.

For international tests we have a relatively small list of judges, and when members of such a panel arrive at an event they usually know each other and can discuss, if they have not done so in the past, their respective points of view and ways of judging certain movements, and so some common guidelines can be established. In local competitions this is impossible, at least in practice, which is a pity; for it would be most desirable in the elementary tests to have a panel of first-rate judges who could set the young riders onto the right track from the start.

I grant you that judges are not always perfect but perhaps the day will come when we shall have official examinations recognizing only truly qualified judges. By doing so we may then be able to produce unity in the manner of training and riding and a correspondingly uniform system of judging and scoring. But even then do not expect judges, any more than riders, to become infallible. Involuntary lapses on both sides are bound to occur. Some movements come in swift sequels and must be scored very rapidly, requiring the practised, keen eye, the 'judging reflexes', in fact, which are the mirror of the 'riding reflexes' you, on the other side of the white fence, must learn to develop.

There is a further contribution that the judges could make right now to help competitors. Aside from jotting down their scores and a few observations in the space reserved for such remarks, they should not only be available to answer questions after the test, but should take the initiative in explaining their judgments; commenting on the individual tests, underscoring what was best and what was worst; pointing out the causes of shortcomings and advising on the means to remedy them. The reasonable rider will not mind a measure of harsh criticism, as long as it is constructive, and only by this method will the true purpose of the dressage test, as an aid towards perfection, be served.

Of course it is nice to be first, and it is natural and right that this should be the objective, but there is more than this in competition. Whatever our final position, we should not forget that we enter tests to get an evaluation of our home-work, a measuring of our progress. Thus the dressage test is both an end and a means.

But even the colour of our rosettes may be somewhat misleading. I am the first to say that 'it is a poor workman who always blames his tool', but there is not the slightest doubt that some horses make it easier to win on than others. If you are able to improve a rather unpromising horse to the point of being placed near the top of a given test you are more than likely to reach first place when given a chance to ride a better one.

I have wanted to explain these points in order to put into perspective the discouragement which I know can lurk in the four corners of dressage arenas and can so easily affect the young competitor. A famous judge and examiner whom I knew well used to say: "I'll give you twenty-four hours after the test to curse your judges, but then get back to work.' If you want to make progress, be persevering, open to criticism and wary of praise.

INDEX

WILSHIRE HORSE LOVERS' LIBRARY

The books listed above can be obtained from your book dealer or directly from Melvin Powers. When ordering, please remit $2.00 postage for the first book and $1.00 for each additional book.

Melvin Powers
12015 Sherman Road, No. Hollywood, California 91605

A NOTE FROM THE PUBLISHER

Because the opinions of our readers play an important part in our publishing decisions, we would appreciate your answering the following questions:

Did you enjoy reading this book? Why?
Which ideas in the book impressed you most?
How do you plan to incorporate these ideas into your daily life?

Send to:

Melvin Powers
Wilshire Book Company
12015 Sherman Road
No. Hollywood, CA 91605-3781

We would be pleased to send you a current catalog of our self-help books. Mail your request to Customer Service at the address above or fax it to (818) 765-2922.

Although we publish books in many categories, we are best known for our motivational and inspirational books, such as *Psycho-Cybernetics* by Maxwell Maltz, M.D., *Think & Grow Rich* by Napoleon Hill, and *The Magic of Thinking Success* by David Schwartz, Ph.D. If you have an idea for a book or have a manuscript in progress, you are welcome to write me, or you may call me at (818) 765-8579 to discuss your project.

MELVIN POWERS SELF-IMPROVEMENT LIBRARY

ASTROLOGY

____ASTROLOGY—HOW TO CHART YOUR HOROSCOPE Max Heindel 7.00
____ASTROLOGY AND SEXUAL ANALYSIS Morris C. Goodman 7.00
____ASTROLOGY AND YOU Carroll Righter 5.00
____ASTROLOGY MADE EASY Astarte 7.00
____ASTROLOGY, ROMANCE, YOU AND THE STARS Anthony Norvell 10.00
____MY WORLD OF ASTROLOGY Sydney Omarr 7.00
____THOUGHT DIAL Sydney Omarr 7.00
____WHAT THE STARS REVEAL ABOUT THE MEN IN YOUR LIFE Thelma White 3.00

BRIDGE

____BRIDGE BIDDING MADE EASY Edwin B. Kantar 10.00
____BRIDGE CONVENTIONS Edwin B. Kantar 10.00
____COMPETITIVE BIDDING IN MODERN BRIDGE Edgar Kaplan 7.00
____DEFENSIVE BRIDGE PLAY COMPLETE Edwin B Kantar 20.00
____GAMESMAN BRIDGE—PLAY BETTER WITH KANTAR Edwin B. Kantar 7.00
____HOW TO IMPROVE YOUR BRIDGE Alfred Sheinwold 7.00
____IMPROVING YOUR BIDDING SKILLS Edwin B. Kantar 7.00
____INTRODUCTION TO DECLARER'S PLAY Edwin B. Kantar 7.00
____INTRODUCTION TO DEFENDER'S PLAY Edwin B. Kantar 7.00
____KANTAR FOR THE DEFENSE Edwin B. Kantar 7.00
____KANTAR FOR THE DEFENSE VOLUME 2 Edwin B. Kantar 7.00
____TEST YOUR BRIDGE PLAY Edwin B. Kantar 7.00
____VOLUME 2—TEST YOUR BRIDGE PLAY Edwin B. Kantar 10.00
____WINNING DECLARER PLAY Dorothy Hayden Truscott 10.00

BUSINESS, STUDY & REFERENCE

____BRAINSTORMING Charles Clark 10.00
____CONVERSATION MADE EASY Elliot Russell 5.00
____EXAM SECRET Dennis B. Jackson 5.00
____FIX-IT BOOK Arthur Symons 2.00
____HOW TO DEVELOP A BETTER SPEAKING VOICE M. Hellier 5.00
____HOW TO SAVE 50% ON GAS & CAR EXPENSES Ken Stansbie 5.00
____HOW TO SELF-PUBLISH YOUR BOOK & MAKE IT A BEST SELLER Melvin Powers . . 20.00
____INCREASE YOUR LEARNING POWER Geoffrey A. Dudley 5.00
____PRACTICAL GUIDE TO BETTER CONCENTRATION Melvin Powers 5.00
____PUBLIC SPEAKING MADE EASY Thomas Montalbo 10.00
____7 DAYS TO FASTER READING William S. Schaill 7.00
____SONGWRITER'S RHYMING DICTIONARY Jane Shaw Whitfield 10.00
____SPELLING MADE EASY Lester D. Basch & Dr. Milton Finkelstein 3.00
____STUDENT'S GUIDE TO BETTER GRADES J.A. Rickard 3.00
____TEST YOURSELF—FIND YOUR HIDDEN TALENT Jack Shafer 3.00
____YOUR WILL & WHAT TO DO ABOUT IT Attorney Samuel G. King 7.00

CALLIGRAPHY

____ADVANCED CALLIGRAPHY Katherine Jeffares 7.00
____CALLIGRAPHY—THE ART OF BEAUTIFUL WRITING Katherine Jeffares 7.00
____CALLIGRAPHY FOR FUN & PROFIT Anne Leptich & Jacque Evans 7.00
____CALLIGRAPHY MADE EASY Tina Serafini 7.00

CHESS & CHECKERS

____BEGINNER'S GUIDE TO WINNING CHESS Fred Reinfeld 7.00
____CHESS IN TEN EASY LESSONS Larry Evans 10.00
____CHESS MADE EASY Milton L. Hanauer 5.00
____CHESS PROBLEMS FOR BEGINNERS Edited by Fred Reinfeld 5.00

____CHESS TACTICS FOR BEGINNERS Edited by Fred Reinfeld 7.00
____HOW TO WIN AT CHECKERS Fred Reinfeld 5.00
____1001 BRILLIANT WAYS TO CHECKMATE Fred Reinfeld 10.00
____1001 WINNING CHESS SACRIFICES & COMBINATIONS Fred Reinfeld 10.00

COOKERY & HERBS

____CULPEPER'S HERBAL REMEDIES Dr. Nicholas Culpeper 5.00
____FAST GOURMET COOKBOOK Poppy Cannon 2.50
____HEALING POWER OF HERBS May Bethel 5.00
____HEALING POWER OF NATURAL FOODS May Bethel 7.00
____HERBS FOR HEALTH—HOW TO GROW & USE THEM Louise Evans Doole 7.00
____HOME GARDEN COOKBOOK—DELICIOUS NATURAL FOOD RECIPES Ken Kraft 3.00
____MEATLESS MEAL GUIDE Tomi Ryan & James H. Ryan, M.D. 4.00
____VEGETABLE GARDENING FOR BEGINNERS Hugh Wilberg 2.00
____VEGETABLES FOR TODAY'S GARDENS R. Milton Carleton 2.00
____VEGETARIAN COOKERY Janet Walker 10.00
____VEGETARIAN COOKING MADE EASY & DELECTABLE Veronica Vezza 3.00

GAMBLING & POKER

____HOW TO WIN AT POKER Terence Reese & Anthony T. Watkins 7.00
____SCARNE ON DICE John Scarne 15.00
____WINNING AT CRAPS Dr. Lloyd T. Commins 5.00
____WINNING AT GIN Chester Wander & Cy Rice 3.00
____WINNING AT POKER—AN EXPERT'S GUIDE John Archer 10.00
____WINNING AT 21—AN EXPERT'S GUIDE John Archer 7.00

HEALTH

____BEE POLLEN Lynda Lyngheim & Jack Scagnetti 5.00
____COPING WITH ALZHEIMER'S Rose Oliver, Ph.D. & Francis Bock, Ph.D. ... 10.00
____DR. LINDNER'S POINT SYSTEM FOOD PROGRAM Peter G Lindner, M.D. 2.00
____HELP YOURSELF TO BETTER SIGHT Margaret Darst Corbett 7.00
____HOW YOU CAN STOP SMOKING PERMANENTLY Ernest Caldwell 5.00
____MIND OVER PLATTER Peter G Lindner, M.D. 5.00
____NATURE'S WAY TO NUTRITION & VIBRANT HEALTH Robert J. Scrutton 3.00
____NEW CARBOHYDRATE DIET COUNTER Patti Lopez-Pereira 2.00
____REFLEXOLOGY Dr. Maybelle Segal 5.00
____REFLEXOLOGY FOR GOOD HEALTH Anna Kaye & Don C. Matchan 7.00
____30 DAYS TO BEAUTIFUL LEGS Dr. Marc Selner 3.00
____WONDER WITHIN Thomas S. Coyle, M.D. 10.00
____YOU CAN LEARN TO RELAX Dr. Samuel Gutwirth 5.00

HOBBIES

____BEACHCOMBING FOR BEGINNERS Norman Hickin 2.00
____BLACKSTONE'S MODERN CARD TRICKS Harry Blackstone 7.00
____BLACKSTONE'S SECRETS OF MAGIC Harry Blackstone 7.00
____COIN COLLECTING FOR BEGINNERS Burton Hobson & Fred Reinfeld 7.00
____ENTERTAINING WITH ESP Tony 'Doc' Shiels 2.00
____400 FASCINATING MAGIC TRICKS YOU CAN DO Howard Thurston 7.00
____HOW I TURN JUNK INTO FUN AND PROFIT Sari 3.00
____HOW TO WRITE A HIT SONG AND SELL IT Tommy Boyce 10.00
____MAGIC FOR ALL AGES Walter Gibson 7.00
____STAMP COLLECTING FOR BEGINNERS Burton Hobson 3.00

HORSE PLAYER'S WINNING GUIDES

____BETTING HORSES TO WIN Les Conklin 7.00
____ELIMINATE THE LOSERS Bob McKnight 5.00
____HOW TO PICK WINNING HORSES Bob McKnight 5.00
____HOW TO WIN AT THE RACES Sam (The Genius) Lewin 5.00
____HOW YOU CAN BEAT THE RACES Jack Kavanagh 5.00

___ MAKING MONEY AT THE RACES David Barr 7.00
___ PAYDAY AT THE RACES Les Conklin 7.00
___ SMART HANDICAPPING MADE EASY William Bauman 5.00
___ SUCCESS AT THE HARNESS RACES Barry Meadow 7.00

HUMOR
___ HOW TO FLATTEN YOUR TUSH Coach Marge Reardon 2.00
___ JOKE TELLER'S HANDBOOK Bob Orben 7.00
___ JOKES FOR ALL OCCASIONS Al Schock 5.00
___ 2,000 NEW LAUGHS FOR SPEAKERS Bob Orben 7.00
___ 2,400 JOKES TO BRIGHTEN YOUR SPEECHES Robert Orben 7.00
___ 2,500 JOKES TO START'EM LAUGHING Bob Orben 10.00

HYPNOTISM
___ CHILDBIRTH WITH HYPNOSIS William S. Kroger, M.D. 5.00
___ HOW TO SOLVE YOUR SEX PROBLEMS WITH SELF-HYPNOSIS Frank Caprio, M.D. . . 5.00
___ HOW YOU CAN BOWL BETTER USING SELF-HYPNOSIS Jack Heise 7.00
___ HOW YOU CAN PLAY BETTER GOLF USING SELF-HYPNOSIS Jack Heise 3.00
___ HYPNOSIS AND SELF-HYPNOSIS Bernard Hollander, M.D. 7.00
___ HYPNOTISM (Originally published 1893) Carl Sextus 5.00
___ HYPNOTISM MADE EASY Dr. Ralph Winn 7.00
___ HYPNOTISM MADE PRACTICAL Louis Orton 5.00
___ HYPNOTISM REVEALED Melvin Powers 3.00
___ HYPNOTISM TODAY Leslie LeCron & Jean Bordeaux, Ph.D. 5.00
___ MODERN HYPNOSIS Lesley Kuhn & Salvatore Russo, Ph.D. 5.00
___ NEW CONCEPTS OF HYPNOSIS Bernard C. Gindes, M.D. 10.00
___ NEW SELF-HYPNOSIS Paul Adams 10.00
___ POST-HYPNOTIC INSTRUCTIONS—SUGGESTIONS FOR THERAPY Arnold Furst . . . 10.00
___ PRACTICAL GUIDE TO SELF-HYPNOSIS Melvin Powers 5.00
___ PRACTICAL HYPNOTISM Philip Magonet, M.D. 3.00
___ SECRETS OF HYPNOTISM S.J. Van Pelt, M.D. 5.00
___ SELF-HYPNOSIS—A CONDITIONED-RESPONSE TECHNIQUE Laurence Sparks 7.00
___ SELF-HYPNOSIS—ITS THEORY, TECHNIQUE & APPLICATION Melvin Powers 3.00
___ THERAPY THROUGH HYPNOSIS Edited by Raphael H. Rhodes 5.00

JUDAICA
___ SERVICE OF THE HEART Evelyn Garfiel, Ph.D. 10.00
___ STORY OF ISRAEL IN COINS Jean & Maurice Gould 2.00
___ STORY OF ISRAEL IN STAMPS Maxim & Gabriel Shamir 1.00
___ TONGUE OF THE PROPHETS Robert St. John 10.00

JUST FOR WOMEN
___ COSMOPOLITAN'S GUIDE TO MARVELOUS MEN Foreword by Helen Gurley Brown . . 3.00
___ COSMOPOLITAN'S HANG-UP HANDBOOK Foreword by Helen Gurley Brown 4.00
___ COSMOPOLITAN'S LOVE BOOK—A GUIDE TO ECSTASY IN BED 7.00
___ COSMOPOLITAN'S NEW ETIQUETTE GUIDE Foreword by Helen Gurley Brown 4.00
___ I AM A COMPLEAT WOMAN Doris Hagopian & Karen O'Connor Sweeney 3.00
___ JUST FOR WOMEN—A GUIDE TO THE FEMALE BODY Richard E. Sand M.D. 5.00
___ NEW APPROACHES TO SEX IN MARRIAGE John E. Eichenlaub, M.D. 3.00
___ SEXUALLY ADEQUATE FEMALE Frank S. Caprio, M.D. 3.00
___ SEXUALLY FULFILLED WOMAN Dr. Rachel Copelan 5.00

MARRIAGE, SEX & PARENTHOOD
___ ABILITY TO LOVE Dr. Allan Fromme 7.00
___ GUIDE TO SUCCESSFUL MARRIAGE Drs. Albert Ellis & Robert Harper 7.00
___ HOW TO RAISE AN EMOTIONALLY HEALTHY, HAPPY CHILD Albert Ellis, Ph.D. 10.00
___ PARENT SURVIVAL TRAINING Marvin Silverman, Ed.D. & David Lustig, Ph.D. 10.00
___ SEX WITHOUT GUILT Albert Ellis, Ph.D. 7.00
___ SEXUALLY ADEQUATE MALE Frank S. Caprio, M.D. 3.00

___ SEXUALLY FULFILLED MAN Dr. Rachel Copelan 5.00
___ STAYING IN LOVE Dr. Norton F. Kristy 7.00

MELVIN POWERS'S MAIL ORDER LIBRARY

___ HOW TO GET RICH IN MAIL ORDER Melvin Powers 20.00
___ HOW TO SELF-PUBLISH YOUR BOOK Melvin Powers 20.00
___ HOW TO WRITE A GOOD ADVERTISEMENT Victor O. Schwab 20.00
___ MAIL ORDER MADE EASY J. Frank Brumbaugh 20.00
___ MAKING MONEY WITH CLASSIFIED ADS Melvin Powers 20.00

METAPHYSICS & OCCULT

___ CONCENTRATION—A GUIDE TO MENTAL MASTERY Mouni Sadhu 7.00
___ EXTRA-TERRESTRIAL INTELLIGENCE—THE FIRST ENCOUNTER 6.00
___ FORTUNE TELLING WITH CARDS P. Foli 5.00
___ HOW TO INTERPRET DREAMS, OMENS & FORTUNE TELLING SIGNS Gettings 5.00
___ HOW TO UNDERSTAND YOUR DREAMS Geoffrey A. Dudley 5.00
___ MAGICIAN—HIS TRAINING AND WORK W.E. Butler 7.00
___ MEDITATION Mouni Sadhu 10.00
___ MODERN NUMEROLOGY Morris C. Goodman 5.00
___ NUMEROLOGY—ITS FACTS AND SECRETS Ariel Yvon Taylor 5.00
___ NUMEROLOGY MADE EASY W. Mykian 5.00
___ PALMISTRY MADE EASY Fred Gettings 5.00
___ PALMISTRY MADE PRACTICAL Elizabeth Daniels Squire 7.00
___ PROPHECY IN OUR TIME Martin Ebon 2.50
___ SUPERSTITION—ARE YOU SUPERSTITIOUS? Eric Maple 2.00
___ TAROT Mouni Sadhu 10.00
___ TAROT OF THE BOHEMIANS Papus 7.00
___ WAYS TO SELF-REALIZATION Mouni Sadhu 7.00
___ WITCHCRAFT, MAGIC & OCCULTISM—A FASCINATING HISTORY W.B. Crow 10.00
___ WITCHCRAFT—THE SIXTH SENSE Justine Glass 7.00

RECOVERY

___ KNIGHT IN RUSTY ARMOR Robert Fisher 5.00
___ KNIGHT IN RUSTY ARMOR (Hard cover edition) Robert Fisher 10.00
___ KNIGHTS WITHOUT ARMOR (Hard cover edition) Aaron R. Kipnis, Ph.D. ... 10.00

SELF-HELP & INSPIRATIONAL

___ CHARISMA—HOW TO GET "THAT SPECIAL MAGIC" Marcia Grad 7.00
___ DAILY POWER FOR JOYFUL LIVING Dr. Donald Curtis 7.00
___ DYNAMIC THINKING Melvin Powers 5.00
___ GREATEST POWER IN THE UNIVERSE U.S. Andersen 10.00
___ GROW RICH WHILE YOU SLEEP Ben Sweetland 10.00
___ GROW RICH WITH YOUR MILLION DOLLAR MIND Brian Adams 7.00
___ GROWTH THROUGH REASON Albert Ellis, Ph.D. 10.00
___ GUIDE TO PERSONAL HAPPINESS Albert Ellis, Ph.D. & Irving Becker, Ed.D. ... 10.00
___ HANDWRITING ANALYSIS MADE EASY John Marley 10.00
___ HANDWRITING TELLS Nadya Olyanova 7.00
___ HOW TO ATTRACT GOOD LUCK A.H.Z. Carr 7.00
___ HOW TO DEVELOP A WINNING PERSONALITY Martin Panzer 7.00
___ HOW TO DEVELOP AN EXCEPTIONAL MEMORY Young & Gibson 10.00
___ HOW TO LIVE WITH A NEUROTIC Albert Ellis, Ph.D. 7.00
___ HOW TO OVERCOME YOUR FEARS M.P. Leahy, M.D. 3.00
___ HOW TO SUCCEED Brian Adams 7.00
___ HUMAN PROBLEMS & HOW TO SOLVE THEM Dr. Donald Curtis 5.00
___ I CAN Ben Sweetland 8.00
___ I WILL Ben Sweetland 10.00
___ KNIGHT IN RUSTY ARMOR Robert Fisher 5.00
___ KNIGHT IN RUSTY ARMOR (Hard Cover) Robert Fisher 10.00
___ LEFT-HANDED PEOPLE Michael Barsley 5.00

____ MAGIC IN YOUR MIND U.S. Andersen 10.00
____ MAGIC OF THINKING SUCCESS Dr. David J. Schwartz 8.00
____ MAGIC POWER OF YOUR MIND Walter M. Germain 10.00
____ MENTAL POWER THROUGH SLEEP SUGGESTION Melvin Powers 3.00
____ NEVER UNDERESTIMATE THE SELLING POWER OF A WOMAN Dottie Walters 7.00
____ NEW GUIDE TO RATIONAL LIVING Albert Ellis, Ph.D. & R. Harper, Ph.D. 10.00
____ PSYCHO-CYBERNETICS Maxwell Maltz, M.D. 7.00
____ PSYCHOLOGY OF HANDWRITING Nadya Olyanova 7.00
____ SALES CYBERNETICS Brian Adams 10.00
____ SCIENCE OF MIND IN DAILY LIVING Dr. Donald Curtis 7.00
____ SECRET OF SECRETS U.S. Andersen 7.00
____ SECRET POWER OF THE PYRAMIDS U.S. Andersen 7.00
____ SELF-THERAPY FOR THE STUTTERER Malcolm Frazer 3.00
____ SUCCESS CYBERNETICS U.S. Andersen 7.00
____ 10 DAYS TO A GREAT NEW LIFE William E. Edwards 3.00
____ THINK AND GROW RICH Napoleon Hill 10.00
____ THINK LIKE A WINNER Walter Doyle Staples, Ph.D. 10.00
____ THREE MAGIC WORDS U.S. Andersen 10.00
____ TREASURY OF COMFORT Edited by Rabbi Sidney Greenberg 10.00
____ TREASURY OF THE ART OF LIVING Sidney S. Greenberg 7.00
____ WHAT YOUR HANDWRITING REVEALS Albert E. Hughes 4.00
____ WONDER WITHIN Thomas F. Coyle, M.D. 10.00
____ YOUR SUBCONSCIOUS POWER Charles M. Simmons 7.00
____ YOUR THOUGHTS CAN CHANGE YOUR LIFE Dr. Donald Curtis 7.00

SPORTS
____ BILLIARDS—POCKET • CAROM • THREE CUSHION Clive Cottingham, Jr. 7.00
____ COMPLETE GUIDE TO FISHING Vlad Evanoff 2.00
____ HOW TO IMPROVE YOUR RACQUETBALL Lubarsky, Kaufman & Scagnetti 5.00
____ HOW TO WIN AT POCKET BILLIARDS Edward D. Knuchell 10.00
____ JOY OF WALKING Jack Scagnetti 3.00
____ LEARNING & TEACHING SOCCER SKILLS Eric Worthington 3.00
____ RACQUETBALL FOR WOMEN Toni Hudson, Jack Scagnetti & Vince Rondone 3.00
____ SECRET OF BOWLING STRIKES Dawson Taylor 5.00
____ SOCCER—THE GAME & HOW TO PLAY IT Gary Rosenthal 7.00
____ STARTING SOCCER Edward F Dolan, Jr. 5.00

TENNIS LOVER'S LIBRARY
____ HOW TO BEAT BETTER TENNIS PLAYERS Loring Fiske 4.00
____ PSYCH YOURSELF TO BETTER TENNIS Dr. Walter A. Luszki 2.00
____ TENNIS FOR BEGINNERS Dr. H.A. Murray 2.00
____ TENNIS MADE EASY Joel Brecheen 5.00
____ WEEKEND TENNIS—HOW TO HAVE FUN & WIN AT THE SAME TIME Bill Talbert ... 3.00

WILSHIRE PET LIBRARY
____ DOG TRAINING MADE EASY & FUN John W. Kellogg 5.00
____ HOW TO BRING UP YOUR PET DOG Kurt Unkelbach 2.00
____ HOW TO RAISE & TRAIN YOUR PUPPY Jeff Griffen 5.00

The books listed above can be obtained from your book dealer or directly from Melvin Powers. When ordering, please remit $2.00 postage for the first book and $1.00 for each additional book.

Melvin Powers
12015 Sherman Road, No. Hollywood, California 91605

HOW TO GET RICH IN MAIL ORDER
by Melvin Powers

1. How to Develop Your Mail Order Expertise 2. How to Find a Unique Product or Service to Sell 3. How to Make Money with Classified Ads 4. How to Make Money with Display Ads 5. The Unlimited Potential for Making Money with Direct Mail 6. How to Copycat Successful Mail Order Operations 7. How I Created A Best Seller Using the Copycat Technique 8. How to Start and Run a Profitable Mail Order, Special Interest Book or Record Business 9. I Enjoy Selling Books by Mail – Some of My Successful and Not-So-Successful Ads and Direct Mail Circulars 10. Five of My Most Successful Direct Mail Pieces That Sold and Are Still Selling Millions of Dollars Worth of Books 11. Melvin Powers' Mail Order Success Strategy – Follow It and You'll Become a Millionaire 12. How to Sell Your Products to Mail Order Companies, Retail Outlets, Jobbers, and Fund Raisers for Maximum Distribution and Profits 13. How to Get Free Display Ads and Publicity That Can Put You on the Road to Riches 14. How to Make Your Advertising Copy Sizzle to Make You Wealthy 15. Questions and Answers to Help You Get Started Making Money in Your Own Mail Order Business 16. A Personal Word from Melvin Powers 17. How to Get Started Making Money in Mail Order. 18. Selling Products on Television - An Exciting Challenge 8½"x11" – 352 Pages...$20.00

HOW TO SELF-PUBLISH YOUR BOOK AND HAVE THE FUN AND EXCITEMENT OF BEING A BEST-SELLING AUTHOR
by Melvin Powers

An expert's step-by-step guide to successfully marketing your book 240 Pages...$20.00

A NEW GUIDE TO RATIONAL LIVING
by Albert Ellis, Ph.D. & Robert A. Harper, Ph.D.

1. How Far Can You Go With Self-Analysis? 2. You Feel the Way You Think 3. Feeling Well by Thinking Straight 4. How You Create Your Feelings 5. Thinking Yourself Out of Emotional Disturbances 6. Recognizing and Attacking Neurotic Behavior 7. Overcoming the Influences of the Past 8. Does Reason Always Prove Reasonable? 9. Refusing to Feel Desperately Unhappy 10. Tackling Dire Needs for Approval 11. Eradicating Dire Fears of Failure 12. How to Stop Blaming and Start Living 13. How to Feel Undepressed though Frustrated 14. Controlling Your Own Destiny 15. Conquering Anxiety 256 Pages...$10.00

PSYCHO-CYBERNETICS
A New Technique for Using Your Subconscious Power
by Maxwell Maltz, M.D., F.I.C.S.

1. The Self Image: Your Key to a Better Life 2. Discovering the Success Mechanism Within You 3. Imagination—The First Key to Your Success Mechanism 4. Dehypnotize Yourself from False Beliefs 5. How to Utilize the Power of Rational Thinking 6. Relax and Let Your Success Mechanism Work for You 7. You Can Acquire the Habit of Happiness 8. Ingredients of the Success-Type Personality and How to Acquire Them 9. The Failure Mechanism: How to Make It Work For You Instead of Against You 10. How to Remove Emotional Scars, or How to Give Yourself an Emotional Face Lift 11. How to Unlock Your Real Personality 12. Do-It-Yourself Tranquilizers 288 Pages...$7.00

A PRACTICAL GUIDE TO SELF-HYPNOSIS
by Melvin Powers

1. What You Should Know About Self-Hypnosis 2. What About the Dangers of Hypnosis? 3. Is Hypnosis the Answer? 4. How Does Self-Hypnosis Work? 5. How to Arouse Yourself from the Self-Hypnotic State 6. How to Attain Self-Hypnosis 7. Deepening the Self-Hypnotic State 8. What You Should Know About Becoming an Excellent Subject 9. Techniques for Reaching the Somnambulistic State 10. A New Approach to Self-Hypnosis When All Else Fails 11. Psychological Aids and Their Function 12. The Nature of Hypnosis 13. Practical Applications of Self-Hypnosis 128 Pages...$5.00

The books listed above can be obtained from your book dealer or directly from Melvin Powers. When ordering, please remit $2.00 postage for the first book and $1.00 for each additional book.

Melvin Powers
12015 Sherman Road, No. Hollywood, California 91605

Notes

Notes